SPICES

Allspice
56, 96, 125, 144

Asafoetida
59

Berbere spice
117

Black mustard seeds
42, 59, 72, 110, 163

Caraway seeds
149

Cardamom pods
16, 71, 110, 125, 157, 188, 217

Chaat masala
32

Chile flakes
27, 36, 38, 44, 52, 68, 76, 83, 86, 105, 114, 145, 150, 157, 165, 188, 236

Chile powder
105

Chiles
15, 32, 38, 42, 44, 52, 56, 59, 72, 76, 92, 96, 105, 110, 120, 125, 127, 136, 143, 145, 146, 149, 153, 154, 163, 165, 169, 184, 193, 200, 236

Cinnamon
41, 56, 59, 110, 127, 144, 157, 212, 224

Cloves
16, 59, 110, 212

Coriander seeds
15, 16, 48, 68, 75, 83, 105, 128, 165

Cumin
16, 27, 38, 52, 59, 64, 68, 71, 72, 83, 84, 92, 105, 110, 125, 141, 144, 149, 153, 157, 163, 188, 196, 200

Curry leaves
42, 92, 163

Curry powder
38, 179

Fennel seeds
95, 166

SPICES (CONTINUED)

Fenugreek seeds
16

Garam masala
42, 72, 154, 163

Nigella seeds
165

Nutmeg
91, 224

Paprika
27, 78, 146, 150, 158, 200

Peppercorns
95, 110

Saffron
71, 75

Star anise
41, 44, 125, 127, 204, 240

Sumac
52, 119, 131, 170

Szechuan peppercorns
44

Turmeric
16, 32, 34, 38, 42, 59, 64, 68, 71, 72, 92, 105, 141, 154, 157, 163, 196

Za'atar
27, 28, 119, 141, 182

OTK

OTK

OTTOLENGHI TEST KITCHEN

SHELF LOVE

Recipes to Unlock the Secrets of Your Pantry, Fridge, and Freezer

Noor Murad & Yotam Ottolenghi

Photography by Elena Heatherwick

appetite

Contents

Introduction

THE ARCHES

There's a railway arch in north London, built from equal parts brick and tahini, walls coated in olive oil and floors stained with spice: habanero and fenugreek, Aleppo chile and black lime. To the outsider it is identified through stacks of wooden pallets, blue shutters, red brick, and industrial steel, easily missed and effortlessly unglamorous. To the insider, it's a tiny bit more. This is the Ottolenghi Test Kitchen, the OTK to some, where a stripped-back railway arch makes absolute sense, where a group of individuals meet and eat, cook and write, tear and share, and gather with just one motive: to create good food with good ingredients, and to share it with the world.

THE TEAM

Those who know us will tell you that Yotam Ottolenghi and his Test Kitchen colleagues are an eccentric bunch, our various backgrounds and stories leading us to this one shared space. To say that the Test Kitchen can be narrowed down to one voice would be inaccurate, really, when it is in fact a collection of voices and personalities, the comings and goings of chefs and writers, of food stylists and photographers, of sommeliers and every other talent in the trade. It is a decade of collected fingerprints, the kind of space you walk into and know, "This place is greater than the sum of its parts."

Leading the crew you have Noor Murad, who informally crowns herself the queen of Middle Eastern feasts; Verena Lochmuller, who is basically the Google search engine to all baking questions; Ixta Belfrage, co-author of *Flavor* and our inside scoop to the latest foodie trends; Tara Wigley, the in-house word wizard; and, of course, Gitai Fisher, the man who keeps us all in check while making absolutely sure we stay out of trouble. There's also our trusted colleague Claudine Boulstridge, our secret OTK weapon, who tries and tests all of our recipes from her family kitchen in Wales. The latest addition to our team of misfits is Chaya Pugh, who joined just as the book was coming together, adding heaped spoonfuls of spicy personality to the brew. Ultimately, of course, there is Big Y, as we dub him, who pushes and inspires us, while making sure we have enough wiggle room to sail our own course. Our stories are sprinkled across this book, written and narrated by Noor, whose Middle Eastern influence makes a prominent mark on these pages.

THE STORY

The year is 2020. It doesn't need an introduction, more of an acknowledgment, that this is the year in which the rug was pulled out from under the world's feet. Suddenly, and blindly, we found

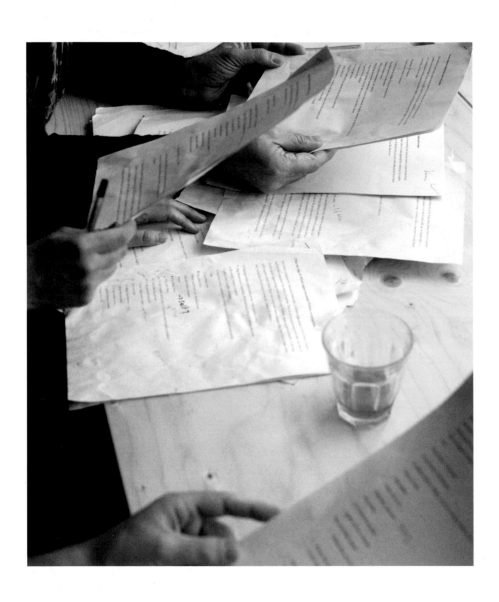

ourselves dispersed and separated, across borders and continents alike. Unstable ground had us grabbing for what was true and familiar and, to no surprise, all steps led to our kitchens. We did what we all do best, and began creating recipes based on what we had in our cabinets and fridges, our freezers and pantries. We grabbed and raided and rummaged and emptied. We stripped down our kitchens to build up our tables and soon realized that any recipe—any food, any dish—can be made unequivocally "Ottolenghi" with the right know-how, the right willingness to work with what you have.

So 2020, the most momentous of all years, brought with it the first OTK cookbook, the one in which we teach you a skill or two that we've recently learned—how to cleverly utilize your kitchen finds while putting a delicious meal on the table. We see it as the first of many stories the Ottolenghi Test Kitchen has to tell, tales of other timely skills that are yet to reveal themselves, accounts of our food adventures and all the little discoveries that we're so desperate to share with you.

THE BOOK

For the longest time, we called this book "Stripped"; we thought of it as a stripping down of our shelves, pantries, cupboards, fridges, and freezers. It felt like a liberation, getting rid of the old to make way for the new. In turn, we wanted to set the foundations and framework in place for you to flex your own creativity, stripping down your own kitchens, raiding your own shelves and swapping things out with your own pantry ingredients. This decluttering approach was freeing, teaching us how to love our kitchens and our stoves, but most importantly teaching us how to love ourselves at an otherwise very challenging time. And so *Shelf Love* (thank you, Caz!), was born, a whimsical description, yes, but also a truly accurate one.

To build up this book we have broken down our kitchens: pulling ingredients apart only to put them back together again—cohesive dishes based on kitchen finds. A bag of dried chickpeas, repurposed. A pound of onions, cooked down. Some wonky-looking vegetables, grilled. There is a "this for that" ethos here; the understanding that, in this new world, the need to improvise, to roll with the punches, is more crucial than ever before.

We carry this ethos throughout the book, as we map out our recipes based on kitchen logistics: from fridge to pantry to one-dish bakes and sweet, sweet endings. It's food that we'd cook at home, for our friends and families, comforting but with a slight edge, a little twist, a "cheffy" addition. They're recipes with stories and personalities, with swap-outs and suggestions, recipes that say without saying, "I'll show you the rules, but here's how to break them." We want you to take these recipes and make them your own, turning this cookbook into a handbook—one to write and scribble on, to stain with turmeric and fold down pages. We want this book to be *that* book, the most haggard-looking book on your shelves, indicating that it serves its purpose and then some. We want, more than anything, for you to show this book some love. Shelf Love.

THAT ONE SHELF IN THE

BACK OF YOUR PANTRY

That one shelf in the back of your pantry

Sitting on that one shelf in the very back of the pantry, all the way to the right, behind the cans, you'll find a forgotten bag of . . . mung beans? Whole wheat flour? Polenta? The beauty in a shelf is that no two are identical, with each turning up with something different to show. Some of them are can-heavy, others full of jars or dried legumes, and some filled to the brim with every pasta shape known to man. Perhaps it's knowing that pantry ingredients have a very long shelf-life, which means there's no real rush to use them until the inevitable clear-out, the "I'm so sure I had some couscous around here somewhere" moment. But the day you do finally get around to decluttering is a day filled with infinite opportunities for reinvention.

Some of our favorite pairings at the Test Kitchen have come from a quick brainstorm and a good rummage through our cabinets: semolina with coconut, black lime with feta, butter beans (lima beans) with preserved lemon. We go in with the mindset that the only limitations in food are the ones we set for ourselves, that rules are meant to be broken, and that everything works unless proven otherwise. After that it's a balancing act, finding that happy medium between what we envision and what we already know. If there's one thing our very interconnected world has taught us it's this: whatever it is, it's probably already been done—the key is to find new ways to speak with food, while still paying tribute to the culture (or cultures) the recipe was inspired by. This often leads to dishes that are familiar, but also not: take tabbouleh and turn it into a fritter (p. 56), eat porridge but make it savory (p. 36), load a French onion soup with chickpeas and warming spices (p. 16). Sometimes, though, it's all about meeting a dish where it's at, and resisting the urge to re-create it: see creamy dreamy hummus (p. 20).

The premise of this book is built on a shelf raid, as is evident throughout this chapter, but really it moves beyond that. On the one hand, shelf clear-outs lead you to become more resourceful with your meals, while, on the other, they create a blank slate for you to refill and restock. Recent times have been all about that: out with the old and in with the new, stripping it all down to build it back up, removing what once was to introduce what now is. This chapter is dedicated to the "out," the "strip," and the "remove," which in turn creates room to play.

(One jar of) butter beans with preserved lemon, chile, and herb oil

Prep time: *20 minutes*
Cook time: *40 minutes*

Butter beans (lima beans) are given the superstar treatment with this preserved lemon, chile, and herb oil. The longer the beans sit in the oil, the better they become, so feel free to make these the day before, allowing them to become wonderful little sponges overnight. Be sure to use good-quality jarred or canned butter beans here; it'll make all the difference. Serve with crusty bread to mop it all up, and maybe some broiled manouri or halloumi.

Serves 4, as part of a mezze spread

5 garlic cloves, *finely chopped*

2 small Fresno chiles, *finely chopped, seeds and all (3 tbsp/30g)*

1 tbsp coriander seeds, *finely crushed with a mortar and pestle*

3 preserved lemons *(3 oz/80g), inner parts discarded and skin finely sliced (¼ cup/45g)*

1½ tbsp roughly chopped thyme leaves

4 rosemary sprigs

1 tbsp tomato paste

¾ cup/180ml olive oil

25 oz/700g canned or jarred butter beans (lima beans) *(we like the Brindisa brand), drained (19 oz/550g)*

2 large vine tomatoes *(8 oz/220g), roughly grated (p. 88) and skins discarded (⅔ cup/120g)*

flaked sea salt and black pepper

1. Put the first eight ingredients and 1¼ teaspoons of flaked salt into a medium sauté pan on medium-low heat and stir everything together. Heat gently for 25 minutes, or until very fragrant but not at all browned. If the oil gets too hot, turn the heat down to low. Stir in the butter beans, then turn the heat up to medium and cook for 10 minutes. Remove from the heat and allow to infuse for at least 1 hour, or longer if time allows.

2. Meanwhile, mix the grated tomato with ¼ teaspoon of flaked sea salt and a good grind of pepper.

3. To serve, pour the butter bean mixture into a shallow bowl and spoon the grated tomato over the top, mixing it in in places.

Make it your own:
– Swap out the butter beans for cannellini beans or chickpeas.
_____
_____
_____

Hawaij onion and chickpea soup with cheesy toast

Prep time: *30 minutes*
Cook time: *1 hour 50 minutes*

This is based on French onion soup. Similar to the classic, a large quantity of onions is cooked low and slow (use a food processor or mandolin to help you slice them), but everything else from that point on is a deviation. Hawaij is a Yemeni spice blend that complements the sweet onions, adding complexity and warmth, and the chickpeas add bulk, making this a meal in a bowl. The cheesy toast is optional but . . . it is melty cheese on crunchy toast after all, and we really think you should make it.

Serves 4, generously

¼ cup/50g unsalted butter

2 tbsp olive oil

2½ lb/1.2kg onions *(about 7–8), halved and thinly sliced*

1 cup/250g uncooked tomato purée

1½ cups/30g fresh cilantro, *roughly chopped*

1 (15 oz/425g) can of chickpeas, *drained (8½ oz/240g)*

6⅓ cups/1.5 liters chicken or vegetable stock

salt and black pepper

SPICE MIX

1 tbsp coriander seeds

2 tsp cumin seeds

2 whole cloves

8 cardamom pods, *shells discarded and seeds reserved*

½ tsp fenugreek seeds

½ tsp ground turmeric

CHEESY TOAST (OPTIONAL)

2 cups/220g coarsely grated mature cheddar

½ cup/10g fresh cilantro, *roughly chopped*

1 large garlic clove, *minced*

6 slices of sourdough, *cut about ¾ inch/2cm thick*

1 tbsp unsalted butter, *at room temperature*

1 tbsp Dijon mustard

1. Put the butter and oil into a large cast-iron saucepan on medium-high heat. Once hot, stir in the onions, then turn the heat down to medium and cook, gently, for 1 hour, stirring only every 10 minutes or so. You want the onions to completely soften and turn golden.

2. Meanwhile, make the spice mix. Put the coriander and cumin seeds, cloves, cardamom, and fenugreek into a small frying pan and place it on medium-high heat. Toast for 5 minutes, then blitz in a spice grinder to a smooth powder (or use a mortar and pestle). Stir in the turmeric and set aside.

3. When the onions are ready, turn the heat to medium-high. Add the spice mix, tomato purée, and cilantro and cook for 5 minutes, stirring occasionally. Add the chickpeas, stock, 1¾ teaspoons of salt, and a very generous amount of black pepper and bring to a boil. Turn the heat to medium and simmer, stirring occasionally, for 30 minutes.

4. For the cheesy toast, preheat the oven to its highest broil setting. In a small bowl, combine the cheese with the cilantro, garlic, and a good grind of pepper.

5. When the soup is almost ready, place the bread on a parchment-lined baking sheet. Broil for 1 minute, then remove from the oven and flip over. Brush the untoasted side with the softened butter, then the Dijon mustard. Top with the cheese mixture and broil for 3–4 minutes, until golden and bubbly. Cut each slice into three.

6. Divide the soup among four bowls and top with a piece of the cheesy toast, serving any extra cheesy toast alongside.

> **Get ahead:**
> – Make the soup the day ahead; the flavors will only intensify over time.

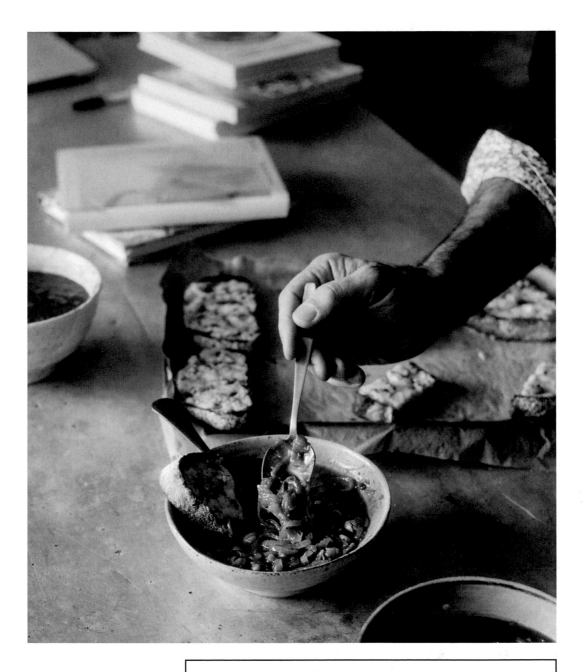

Make it your own:

- Swap out the chickpeas for canned cannellini beans, black-eyed peas, or kidney beans.
- Use any soft herb and a different blend of spices.
- Veganize it: use a vegan cheese, veggie stock, and olive oil in place of butter.

On hummus

Hummus has made its appearance in many an Ottolenghi recipe, and for good reason. It is a universally loved food, so much so that it could practically be its own food group. Recently, Noor wrote a little ode to hummus, sharing her tips, tricks, and hummus hacks, and was amazed at the response. What seemed like second nature to her was not always the case for others and, all of a sudden, hummus regained its rightful place on the throne of foods-we-need-to-continue-talking-about.

A little frustrated at the widespread hummus mishaps, Noor took it upon herself to write a detailed step-by-step guide on how to achieve the ultimate creamy dreamy hummus (p. 20), using both canned and dried chickpeas. "I've come to realize," she wrote, "that you're all a bunch of die-hard hummus lovers and this is the only way to your tahini-laden hearts." Hummus, dear reader, is a science. Go through these tips carefully, pedantic as they may seem, and you will soon be on your way to the creamiest dreamiest hummus that ever did exist.

• If starting with dried chickpeas, be sure to cook them very well. You want them to be very soft, with no bite. If using canned, simmer them in fresh water for a good 15–20 minutes after peeling (step 4)—this will soften them further.

• Use warm chickpeas as these are softer and easier to blend, and are the first step to achieving a smooth hummus with no grit.

• Salt your chickpea water toward the last 15 minutes of cooking time. Also add a pinch of ground cumin to the water, which will give a subtle cumin flavor to your hummus. Save the cooking water. You can use it as a base for soups and stews but, more importantly, you'll be using this flavorful cumin-chickpea water to thin out your hummus.

• Peel your chickpeas (i.e., remove the skins). We know it is a bit of an ask, but it really does make a difference. The chickpeas need to be agitated and there are two ways to do this. Either agitate your cooked chickpeas in their hot water, releasing the skins and using a sieve to scoop and discard those that rise to the surface. Alternatively, and this works best with canned chickpeas, spread them out between two kitchen towels and rub them together, without crushing them. The friction will release the skins, allowing you to easily pick them out and discard them.

• Add a couple of ice cubes to the food processor when blending your hummus. The cold shock of ice against the warm chickpeas will aerate your hummus to wonderful heights.

• Resist the temptation to add olive oil to the base of your hummus. There's plenty of fat in the tahini to give you a beautifully homogenized hummus mixture. Adding olive oil will simply mess with the holy matrimony of chickpea and sesame paste, which you really don't want. Do, however, pour a generous amount of good-quality olive oil on top of the hummus once you've plated it.

• Source the best-quality tahini you can find. We highly recommend tahini made from hulled sesame seeds and light in color, and typically made in the Levant region in countries such as Lebanon or Palestine. Avoid unhulled "sesame pastes" that are dark and gritty. We can't stress enough how important it is to seek out authentic tahini; it really will make or break your hummus. The key to creamy dreamy is in the tahini, really.

Dried vs canned:

In the brave battle of dried vs canned, dried chickpeas won the OTK hummus wars, earning the crown for the creamiest dreamiest hummus, and the hearts of the whole team. It is worth noting, however, that not everyone has the luxury of time to soak dried chickpeas, and we firmly believe that you *can* achieve a close runner-up using canned chickpeas . . . provided you follow our tips and tricks.

Creamy dreamy hummus

Prep time: *10 minutes*
Cook time: *40–90 minutes*
Soaking time (if dried):
overnight

This basic hummus recipe follows the tips and tricks referenced on pp. 18–19. Serve this alongside the pillowy pitas on p. 23.

Serves 6, as part of a mezze spread

**1 cup/200g dried
chickpeas,** *soaked
overnight in plenty of water
and ¾ tsp baking soda*
or
**2 (15 oz/425g) cans of
chickpeas,** *drained
(17 oz/480g total)*
½ tsp baking soda
(if using dried)
salt
1 pinch ground cumin
7–9 tbsp/120–150g tahini
1 garlic clove, *minced,
or more to taste*
1½ tbsp lemon juice,
or more to taste

YOUR CHOICE OF TOPPINGS
olive oil
any chopped herbs
toasted nuts
rose harissa *or your choice of
chile paste*

1. If using dried chickpeas, drain them well after soaking, then put them into a medium saucepan, for which you have a lid, with the ½ tsp baking soda and enough water to cover by about 1½ inches/4cm. Bring to a simmer on medium-high heat, skimming the scum from the surface as needed, then turn the heat down to medium-low, cover with the lid, and simmer from anywhere between 30 and 50 minutes. This will differ greatly depending on your chickpeas, so check them at the 20-minute mark. Toward the last 15 minutes of cooking time, salt the water nicely and add the cumin. Cook the chickpeas until they are very soft.

2. Using a slotted spoon or spider, agitate the chickpeas, giving them a gentle shake in the water, allowing the skins to be released and rise to the surface. Discard the skins (don't worry too much if you don't catch them all). Skip to step 5.

3. If using canned chickpeas, spread them out between two kitchen towels and use your hands to vigorously rub the towels together for a few minutes. Don't press down too hard on the chickpeas; you don't want to crush them. Lift the top towel, to see how you're doing— the friction should have caused the chickpea skins to be released. Discard the skins.

4. Put the canned (and now peeled) chickpeas into a saucepan with enough water to cover, 1 teaspoon of salt, and a pinch of cumin. Simmer for 15 minutes, until soft.

5. Drain the chickpeas over a bowl, saving the water. Put the warm chickpeas into a food processor with 7 tbsp/120g of tahini, the garlic, lemon juice, a couple of ice cubes (scant 1 oz/25g worth), 2 tablespoons of reserved chickpea water and a good pinch of salt. Blitz until smooth(ish), then check on the hummus. You might need more tahini, garlic, lemon, and salt and very likely more chickpea water. Add a bit of each as you need. Don't be shy about adding more tahini—each brand differs and may require you to use more. Blitz the hummus until very smooth, a few minutes at least. Don't worry about the hummus being too loose; it will thicken as it sits.

6. When ready, spread the hummus in a shallow bowl, creating a well in the center. (If not serving right away, store in a sealed container in the fridge for up to 2 days.) Top with a generous glug of olive oil, then personalize your hummus as you wish. We sometimes add herbs, toasted nuts, or rose harissa, but these are just suggestions. Once you get the base right, hummus knows no bounds.

Tinned Chickpeas

Dried Chickpeas

Dried Chickpeas

Tinned Chickpeas

Pita

Prep time: *5 minutes*
Cook time: *40 minutes*
Rising time: *1 hour
20 minutes to overnight*

Up your pita game by making your own: these pitas are light, airy, and pillowy and are the perfect spongy vehicles to stuff, tear, mop, and scoop—making the whole eating experience really very satisfying.

Makes 6 pitas

1 cup/240ml lukewarm water

2 tsp fast-acting dry yeast

2 tsp sugar

2 cups plus 6 tbsp/300g all-purpose flour, *plus extra for dusting*

½ cup/50g whole wheat flour

1 tsp salt

1 tbsp olive oil, *plus extra for oiling*

1. Put the water into a small bowl and sprinkle with the yeast and sugar. Set aside for 5–6 minutes to react and become foamy.

2. Put both flours and the salt into the bowl of a stand mixer, with the dough hook in place, and mix on low speed to combine. Add the olive oil and the yeast mixture, turning the speed to medium-high, and knead for 7 minutes. The dough should be smooth, elastic, and a bit sticky.

3. Transfer the dough to a well-oiled large bowl, cover with a damp kitchen towel, and let rise in a warm place for 1–2 hours, or until doubled in size. Alternatively, let rise, covered and refrigerated, overnight.

4. Transfer the dough to a lightly floured work surface and divide into six 3½ oz/100g pieces. Use your hands to roll each piece into a round ball. Cover with a damp kitchen towel and let rest for 20 minutes.

5. Preheat the oven to 500°F or your highest oven setting. Place a large baking sheet in the oven to warm up.

6. Cut out two pieces of parchment paper roughly the size of your baking sheet, lay them out on your work surface, and sprinkle them with a little flour. Top one piece of paper with two balls of dough, spaced well apart, and use a lightly floured rolling pin to roll each one out into a round, roughly 5 inches/12cm in diameter. Don't tear or overwork the pitas at all, or they won't puff up.

7. Carefully transfer the paper with the two rolled-out rounds to your preheated sheet and bake for 4–5 minutes, or until lightly golden and puffy. Transfer to a clean bowl and cover with a damp kitchen towel to keep warm (save the parchment paper to reuse again). While they're in the oven, prepare the other two rounds in the same way and, when ready, transfer them to the hot sheet and bake in the same way. Continue until you've made six pitas in total. Keep them covered in the bowl until you're ready to serve.

Get ahead:

– Make the dough the night before, letting it rise in the fridge overnight and bringing it back up to room temperature when you're ready to work with it again.
– Freeze the raw dough once you've rolled it into rounds, wrapping it very well before storing it in an airtight container. Defrost before cooking.

Cheesy polenta and tomato sauce

Prep time: *20 minutes*
Cook time: *45 minutes*

This is polenta dressed to impress as a veggie main, but not so overdressed that it can't also work as a side dish, such as to roast chicken or grilled fish. Don't make the polenta until just before you're about to serve, as you don't want it to be completely set.

Serves 4

2 cups/480ml vegetable stock, *or chicken stock, if not veggie*

1½ cups/360ml whole milk

¼ cup/60g unsalted butter

1¼ cups/200g instant polenta

1⅓ cups/150g coarsely grated Gruyère

TOMATO SAUCE

5¼ oz/150g datterini or regular cherry tomatoes

6 tbsp/90ml olive oil

1 onion, *peeled and cut into 8 wedges (5¼ oz/150g)*

6 garlic cloves, *minced*

1 lb 10 oz/750g vine tomatoes, *cored and finely chopped into ½ inch/1cm cubes (seeds and all)*

1 tsp sugar

10 sprigs/5g oregano, *plus 1½ tbsp leaves*

salt and black pepper

1. Place a large sauté pan on high heat and, once very hot, add the datterini/cherry tomatoes and char for 5 minutes. Remove from the pan and set aside, then let the pan cool slightly.

2. Return the pan to medium-high heat along with 4 tablespoons of oil and the onion. Cook for 12 minutes, stirring occasionally, until softened and golden, then add the garlic and cook for 30 seconds more. Add the chopped vine tomatoes, sugar, oregano leaves, 7 tbsp/100ml of water, 1 teaspoon of salt, and plenty of pepper and bring to a boil. Lower the heat to medium and cook for 20 minutes, stirring every now and then, until the tomatoes have started to break down. Add the charred datterini tomatoes and cook for 8 minutes more, until the sauce has thickened. Keep warm on low heat.

3. Heat the remaining 2 tablespoons of oil in a small frying pan on medium-high heat. Add the oregano sprigs and cook for just 1 minute, or until the leaves start to turn a deep green. Set aside.

4. Meanwhile, put the stock, milk, 7 tbsp/100ml of water, half the butter, 1¼ teaspoons of salt, and a good grind of pepper into a medium saucepan on medium-high heat. Bring to a gentle simmer, then turn the heat to medium-low and slowly add the polenta, whisking continuously, until completely incorporated. Continue whisking for 2–3 minutes, until the polenta is cooked and the mixture is quite wet. Stir in the cheese and the remaining butter. Remove from the heat.

5. Spread the polenta out on a large platter. Spoon the tomato sauce on top, gently swirling some into the polenta. Top with the fried oregano and its oil, and serve warm.

Get ahead:
– Make the sauce up to 2 days ahead, warming it through to serve.

Make it your own:
– Play around with different cheeses, herbs, and spices.

_____

_____

Make it your own:

- Play with the beans—we love this with chickpeas too.
- Play with the herbs—use what you have on hand.

_____

_____

Green cannellini and tahini

Prep time: *25 minutes*
Cook time: *40 minutes*

Variations of warm beans served with tahini are popular throughout the Arab world, with dishes such as chickpea fatteh and ful mudammas with tahini at the forefront. Such dishes are typically eaten warm for breakfast, and are a sure way to keep you full until dinner. They're the inspiration for these herby cannellini beans, which can easily be served at any mealtime.

Serves 4 as a main, or 6 as a side

1 round white or brown pita *(3½ oz/100g)*, *pocket opened up, then roughly torn into 1-inch/2.5cm pieces (see p. 23 for homemade pita)*
1 tbsp za'atar
5 tbsp/75ml olive oil
3 (14 oz/400g) cans of cannellini beans, *drained (25 oz/720g total)*
1½ cups/30g parsley, *roughly chopped*
1½ cups/30g cilantro, *roughly chopped*
1 oz/30g chives, *roughly chopped*
1¼ tsp cumin seeds, *toasted and roughly crushed with a mortar and pestle*
1 garlic clove, *minced*
2½ tbsp lemon juice
salt and black pepper

TAHINI SAUCE
rounded ¼ cup/80g tahini
1½ tbsp lemon juice
1 garlic clove, *minced*

CHILE OIL
2½ tbsp olive oil
½ tsp chile flakes
¼ tsp paprika

1. Preheat the oven to 400°F. Toss the pita with the za'atar, 2 tablespoons of oil, ¼ teaspoon of salt, and a good grind of pepper, and spread out on a medium, parchment-lined baking sheet. Bake for 12 minutes, tossing halfway, or until golden and crispy. Set aside to cool.

2. Set aside a mounded ½ cup/100g of the beans in a medium bowl. Put the remaining beans, 2½ cups/600ml of water, and 1 teaspoon of salt into a medium saucepan on medium-high heat. Bring to a boil, then simmer for 15 minutes, or until the beans are nicely softened and warmed through. Keep warm on low heat until ready to serve.

3. Make the tahini sauce by whisking together the tahini, lemon juice, and minced garlic with 5 tablespoons/70ml of water and ¼ teaspoon of salt in a medium bowl, until smooth and pourable. It will thicken as it sits.

4. Make the chile oil by putting the oil and chile flakes into a small frying pan and placing it on medium heat. Cook for 4 minutes, then add the paprika and remove the pan from the heat. Set aside.

5. Put the reserved mounded ½ cup/100g of beans into a food processor, along with the herbs, cumin, garlic, lemon juice, the remaining 3 tablespoons of oil, ⅛ teaspoon salt, and a good grind of pepper. Blitz until smooth, then transfer to a large mixing bowl.

6. Drain the warm beans in a sieve set over a bowl, then add them and 7 tablespoons/100ml of their cooking liquid to the herb mixture, mixing well to combine. You want the beans to be well coated and for the whole mixture to be saucy (but not overly wet), so add a couple of tablespoons more of the cooking liquid if you wish (discarding the remainder).

7. Transfer to a large, lipped platter and drizzle with half the tahini sauce and all the chile oil. Sprinkle with half the pita and serve warm, with the extra tahini and pita alongside.

Za'atar parathas with grated tomato

Prep time: *10 minutes*
Cook time: *1 hour*
Resting time: *20 minutes*

Parathas are flaky South Asian flatbreads—these particular ones are based on Indian laccha paratha, which uses semolina in the dough. There's a bit of a knack to making them but once you get the hang of the process, they are not complicated. Cutting the dough, as we do here, is actually a really simple way of achieving those flaky paratha layers and, once you've mastered the method, they're also quite fun to make! Traditionally there'd be some ghee involved, but we've kept these vegan and also included za'atar and grated tomato, Noor's sneaky additions. Serve these as part of a brunch spread or as a snack.

Makes 6 parathas

2 cups plus 3 tbsp/270g
   all-purpose flour
¼ **cup/40g semolina**
1 **tsp salt**
1 **tsp sugar**
5 **tbsp/75ml olive oil**
½ **cup plus 1–3 tbsp/**
   140–160ml lukewarm
   water
3 **tbsp za'atar**
4 **tbsp vegetable oil,** *plus*
   extra for greasing/oiling

GRATED TOMATO
11¼ **oz/320g vine tomatoes**
   (about 3)
1 **garlic clove,** *minced*
2 **tbsp olive oil**
salt and black pepper

1. Put the flour, semolina, salt, and sugar into a large bowl and use your fingers to mix everything together. Add 1 tablespoon of the olive oil, using your hands to incorporate, then slowly start to pour in the water, using your free hand to bring the dough together into a shaggy mass. Use about ½ cup/120ml of water at first and then slowly add more; you'll use about ½ cup plus 2 tablespoons/155ml in total, give or take. Add a little more if you think it needs it. The mixture will seem quite wet at first, but this is how it should be.

2. Transfer to a clean work surface and knead for 5 minutes, until you have a smooth, pliable dough that isn't at all sticky. Transfer it to a lightly oiled bowl, cover with a damp kitchen towel, and let rest for 20 minutes.

3. Meanwhile, use a box grater to roughly grate the tomatoes (see p. 88), discarding the skins. Transfer the grated tomato to a sieve and allow to drain for about 5 minutes. Put the drained pulp (about 8 oz/220g) into a bowl with the garlic, oil, ¼ teaspoon of salt, and a good grind of pepper. Set aside until needed.

4. Mix together the za'atar and the remaining 4 tablespoons of olive oil in a small bowl.

5. Transfer the dough to a well-oiled surface and divide the mixture into six 3-ounce/80g balls.

6. Working with one piece at a time, and keeping the rest under a damp kitchen towel, use a well-greased rolling pin to roll out the dough as thin as it can go without tearing, paper-thin/1mm thick and about 12 inches/30cm in diameter (it'll start to look a little transparent). Don't worry if it's not a perfect circle; it doesn't need to be.

7. Using a small sharp knife, cut the dough lengthwise into multiple 1/2-inch/1cm-wide strips.

8. Drizzle about 1 tablespoon of the za'atar oil all over the strips, using your hands or the back of a spoon to gently spread it all over the surface.

9. Use your fingers to push the strips together so that you end up with one long piece of dough.

10. Then, using your dominant hand, wind the whole thing around the four fingers of your other hand and tuck the end through the center, to form a round. It will look like a bird's nest. Continue in this way with the remaining dough, making sure your work surface is well oiled each time.

11. Roll out each of the rounds into a 4–5 inch/10–12cm disc.

12. In a medium frying pan on medium heat, cook each paratha for 3 minutes on each side. Brush the top with about 1 teaspoon of vegetable oil, then flip over, cook for another 1 minute, brushing the other side with another 1 teaspoon of oil, flipping again and cooking for a final 1 minute. Place the cooked paratha on a baking sheet or plate and cover with a kitchen towel (this'll help keep it nice and soft). Continue in this way with the rest, using two pans to speed things up.

13. Serve the parathas with the grated tomato alongside.

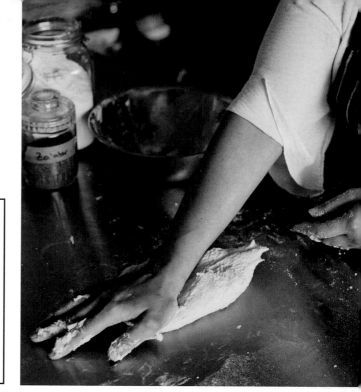

Make it your own:

– Play around with different spices, or make these parathas plain with some ghee instead of the za'atar oil, if you're not vegan.

_____

_____

_____

Chaat masala chickpea and polenta fries

Prep time: *15 minutes*
Cook time: *45 minutes*
Setting time: *30 minutes*

These fries celebrate our favorite little bean in its multiple forms by using chickpea (gram) flour for the base, and then whole chickpeas and chickpea water (aquafaba) for a wonderfully vegan mayo. We love the sour tang you get from the chaat masala here, thanks to the mango powder in this Indian spice mix.

Serves 4, as a snack

1 small red onion, *finely chopped (¾ cup/90g)*

1 tbsp lemon juice

2¼ tsp chaat masala

⅓ tsp ground turmeric

3½ tbsp olive oil

1 cup/100g chickpea (gram) flour

⅔ cup/100g instant polenta

½ cup/10g cilantro, *roughly chopped*

2 small serrano chiles, *finely chopped, seeded if you don't like heat*

salt and black pepper

CHICKPEA MAYO

1 (15 oz/425g) can of chickpeas

1 garlic clove, *minced*

½ tbsp English mustard *(we use Colman's)*

½ tbsp lemon juice

½ cup plus 2 tbsp/150ml vegetable oil

1. Put the onion, lemon juice, and ¼ teaspoon of salt into a small bowl and set aside to pickle and soften.

2. Line an 8-inch/20cm square baking dish with a piece of parchment paper large enough to cover the bottom and sides.

3. Put 2 teaspoons of the chaat masala, all the turmeric, 2 tablespoons of olive oil, 3 cups/700ml of water, 1 teaspoon of salt, and a good grind of pepper into a medium saucepan on medium-high heat. Bring to a simmer, then turn the heat to low. Combine the gram flour and polenta together in a bowl and stir until well combined. Slowly pour this into the seasoned water, whisking continuously to ensure there are no big lumps (there'll still be a few small ones). Cook for 4 minutes, whisking vigorously, until the mixture has thickened and starts to pull away from the sides of the pan. Quickly transfer the mixture to your prepared dish, smoothing out the top with a spatula. Set aside to cool, about 10 minutes, then cover and refrigerate to set for 30 minutes.

4. Make the mayo. Drain the can of chickpeas over a bowl. Measure out ¼ cup/50g of the chickpeas (save the rest for another recipe) and 2½ tablespoons/40ml of the chickpea water (discard the rest). Put the chickpea water, measured-out chickpeas, garlic, mustard, lemon juice, and ⅛ teaspoon of salt into a food processor and blitz until smooth, scraping the sides as you go along. With the motor running, very slowly drizzle in the vegetable oil, until the mixture comes together into a loose mayonnaise-like consistency. Transfer to a small bowl (refrigerate if making ahead).

5. Preheat the oven to 450°F. Transfer the chickpea-polenta mixture from the dish to a cutting board. Trim the edges to give you a neat square, then cut into equal lengths to resemble fries.

6. Spread the chickpea fries out on to a large parchment-lined baking sheet. Drizzle all over with the remaining 1½ tablespoons of olive oil and bake for 25 minutes, turning halfway, until golden and crisp. Pile onto a plate and sprinkle with the remaining ¼ teaspoon of chaat masala and a little salt.

7. Stir the cilantro and chiles into the bowl with the pickled onion and serve this and the mayo alongside.

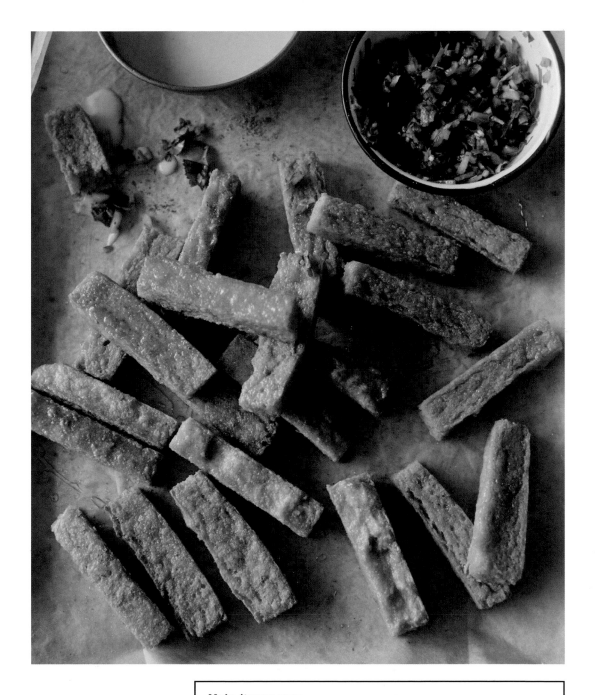

Make it your own:
- If you can't find chaat masala, then mild curry powder works well here too!
- Serve with plain yogurt or store-bought mayo if you like, for non-vegans.

_____

_____

Yellow split pea purée with buttered onions and caper sauce

Prep time: *15 minutes*
Cook time: *1 hour 30 minutes*

Yotam's love affair with the Mediterranean means those signature staples—fatty olive oil, salty feta, briny capers!—permeate both his home kitchen and the OTK. This purée is a take on fava, a Greek mezze dish of yellow split peas with capers and red onion. It's fantastic served as a dip, but also works alongside broiled fish or roasted meat.

Serves 6 as a dip, or 4 as a side

3 tbsp unsalted butter

3 tbsp olive oil

2 red onions, *finely chopped*

1 cup/180g yellow split peas, *rinsed well and drained*

½ tsp ground turmeric

salt

CAPER SAUCE

2 tbsp capers, *roughly chopped*

¼ cup/5g parsley, *finely chopped*

2 thin lemon slices, *seeds discarded and the slices finely chopped (flesh, rind, and all)*

2 tbsp olive oil

1. Put the butter, 2 tablespoons of oil, the onions, and ¾ teaspoon of salt into a large sauté pan, for which you have a lid, on medium heat, and cook for 15–18 minutes, stirring often, until soft and deeply golden. Transfer half the onions, along with most of the oil and melted butter, to a small bowl and set aside, to serve.

2. Add the split peas, turmeric, 5 cups/1.2 liters of water, and ¾ teaspoon of salt to the pan with the remaining onions and bring to a simmer on medium-high heat. Lower the heat to medium and cook for 20 minutes, uncovered. Cover with the lid and cook for another 40–45 minutes, or until the split peas are very soft and most of the liquid has evaporated.

3. Meanwhile, combine all the ingredients for the caper sauce together in a small bowl.

4. While the split peas are still warm, put them, together with any remaining cooking water and the last 1 tablespoon of oil, into a food processor and blitz until completely smooth.

5. Spoon into a shallow dish, creating a dip in the middle. Mix the buttered onions with the caper sauce, then spoon on to the dip. Serve warm, or at room temperature.

Make it your own:
- Veganize it: swap the butter for olive oil.

_____

_____

_____

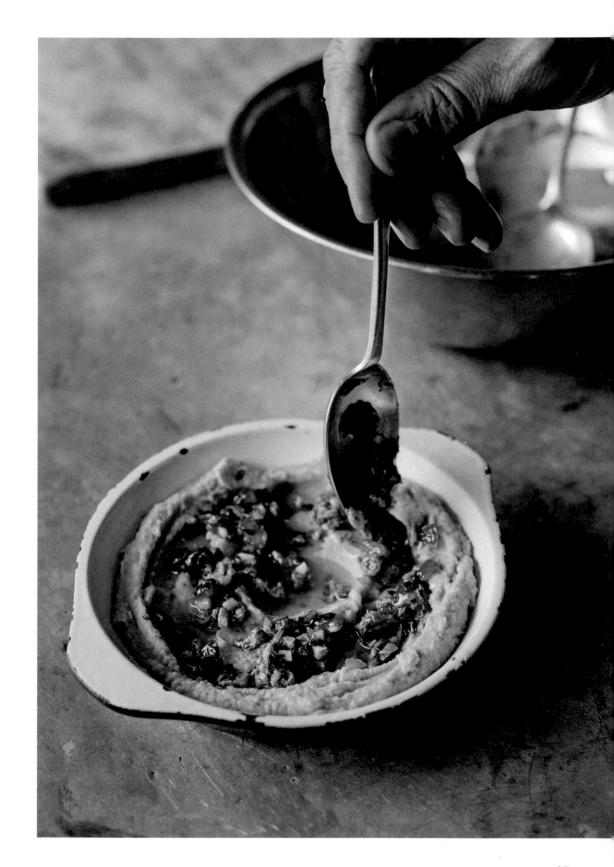

Savory oat porridge
with ginger-garlic crumbs

Prep time: *10 minutes*
Cook time: *35 minutes*

Breakfasts are a solo affair at the OTK, with each person left to their own devices. Tara with her big ol' bowl of eggs and greens, Ixta and Noor with their "every green" green smoothies, and Gitai with his one-cup-of-coffee-in-silence, please. Verena will, more times than not, rustle up a bowl of porridge, sweet spices and raisins stirred in, warm and inviting and easy on the tummy.

This porridge gets a savory twist, thanks to the addition of an umami-rich soy butter and crispy ginger-garlic yumbits. Feel free to quadruple the amount of said yumbits—they're so good sprinkled onto eggs, rice and every other food group (we think).

Serves 4, for breakfast or brunch

12 green onions, *trimmed and halved lengthwise* (6⅓ oz/180g)

3 tbsp olive oil

3 oz/80g fresh ginger, *peeled and finely grated*

12 garlic cloves (about 1 head), *minced*

4 large eggs

1¾ cups/160g rolled oats (gluten-free if you wish)

2 tbsp soy sauce

¼ cup/50g unsalted butter, *fridge cold and cut into ¾-inch/2cm cubes*

1 tsp chile flakes, *or more if you like extra heat*

salt and black pepper

1. Toss the green onions in a bowl with 1 tablespoon of oil and a pinch each of salt and pepper. Place a large, nonstick sauté pan on high heat and, once hot, cook half the green onions for 3 minutes, turning a couple of times, until softened and charred. Transfer to a plate and char the remaining half, adding to the plate when done. Let the pan cool slightly.

2. Wipe out the pan and place it on medium heat with the remaining 2 tablespoons of oil. Once hot, add the ginger and garlic and cook for 15 minutes, stirring occasionally, until deeply golden and crispy. Transfer two-thirds of this mixture to a small bowl and leave the rest in the pan.

3. Meanwhile, boil the eggs for 6 minutes, until soft-boiled (or longer if preferred). Drain, peel, and set aside.

4. To the ginger-garlic pan add the oats, 1 quart/1 liter of water, 1 teaspoon of salt, and a good grind of pepper. Bring to a gentle simmer on medium-high heat, then cook for about 4 minutes, stirring occasionally, until you have a loose porridge. Add a splash more water if needed.

5. Meanwhile, put the soy sauce and a generous amount of pepper into a small saucepan and bring to a simmer on medium-high heat. Turn the heat down to low and slowly whisk in the butter cubes, 2–3 at a time, waiting until just melted before adding some more. Continue in this way until you have a homogenized mixture. Don't let it boil at all as it will split.

6. Divide the porridge among four bowls. Top each bowl with some of the soy butter and green onions. Cut the eggs in half, sprinkle with salt and pepper, and place on top. Finish with the reserved ginger-garlic crumbs and a sprinkling of chile flakes. Serve warm.

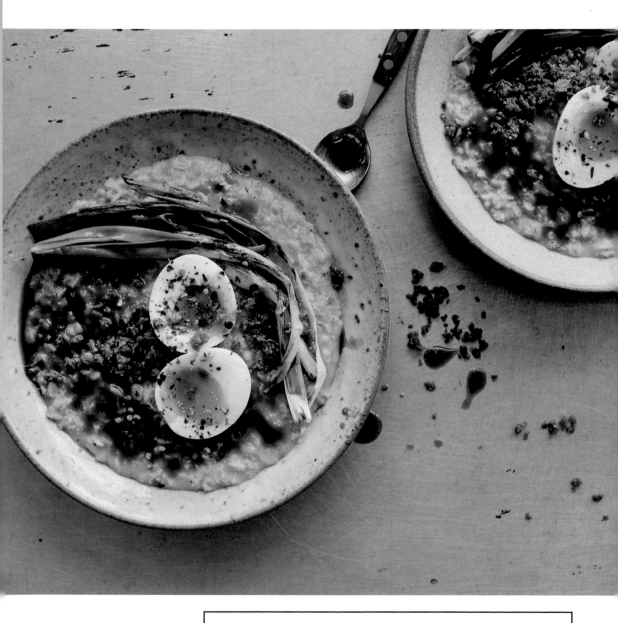

Make it your own:

– Skip the charred green onions and just add some fresh herbs.
– Bulk out your porridge by topping with leftover cooked veggies.
– Make it gluten-free by swapping out the soy with tamari or coconut aminos.

_____

_____

Tamarind, greens, and mung beans with turmeric oil

Prep time: *30 minutes*
Cook time: *1 hour 20 minutes*
Soaking time: *1 hour +*

Thanks to Bahera Agahi for the inspiration for this dish, a lady well versed in the art of Persian cooking. When asked for a recipe, Bahera chuckled and said, "I measure by hand and cook by eye and this is how a dish is made." Noor watched Bahera cook that day, with a mental note to bring this dish to life at the test kitchen. Serve with fluffy white rice, for a complete meal.

Serves 4

7 tbsp/105ml olive oil

2 large onions, *halved and thinly sliced (15 oz/420g)*

10 garlic cloves, *5 minced and 5 thinly sliced*

2 small serrano chiles, *finely chopped, seeds and all (2½ tbsp/25g)*

2 tsp cumin seeds, *roughly crushed with a mortar and pestle*

1 tsp mild curry powder

1 tbsp tomato paste

mounded ½ cup/120g dried green mung beans, *soaked in plenty of cold water for at least 1 hour, then drained*

2 lb 2 oz/1kg Swiss chard, *stalks reserved for another use and leaves roughly torn (1 lb 1 oz/480g)*

1 tsp sugar

3 tbsp tamarind paste

2 cups/40g cilantro, *roughly chopped, plus a handful of extra leaves to serve*

½ tsp ground turmeric

½ tsp chile flakes *(optional)*

½ lemon

½ cup/130g Greek yogurt

salt and black pepper

1. Heat 4 tablespoons of oil in a large sauté pan, for which you have a lid, on medium-high heat. Add the onions and cook for 15–18 minutes, stirring occasionally, until softened and deeply browned. Transfer a third of the onions to a bowl and set aside. To the pan, add the minced garlic, chiles, spices, and tomato paste and cook for another 1 minute. Add the drained mung beans and 3⅓ cups/800ml of water and bring to a boil. Turn the heat down to medium, cover with the lid, and let simmer gently, stirring occasionally, for about 30–35 minutes, or until the mung beans have softened but still retain their shape.

2. Add the Swiss chard, sugar, 1 teaspoon of salt, and a good grind of pepper, then replace the lid and cook for another 10 minutes. Remove the lid and cook for 10 minutes more, or until the chard has softened and the liquid has thickened. Stir in the tamarind and cilantro and keep warm until ready to serve.

3. Toward the last 10 minutes of cooking, put the remaining 3 tablespoons of oil and the sliced garlic into a small frying pan and place it on medium heat. Cook, stirring occasionally, until the garlic is lightly golden, about 12 minutes. Add the turmeric and chile flakes, if using, and remove from the heat.

4. Transfer the mung bean mixture to a large shallow bowl and squeeze the lemon half over the top. Top with spoonfuls of the yogurt, followed by the reserved onions, then spoon on the crispy garlic and its oil. Lastly, garnish with the handful of cilantro leaves and serve warm.

Make it your own:

– Swap out the chard for spinach or other leafy greens.
– Veganize it: leave out the yogurt or use a non-dairy
  alternative.

_____

_____

Soda bread with figs, star anise, and orange

Prep time: *15 minutes*
Cook time: *1 hour*
Cooling time: *45 minutes*

One loaf, no yeast, no fuss, no rising time; everyone needs a foolproof soda bread recipe in their repertoire. We've taken a bit of a sweet approach here, marrying figs together with sweet star anise and cinnamon. To balance this out, serve with softened and nicely salted butter and some bitter marmalade if you like.

Serves 6

¾ cup/180ml whole milk

¾ cup plus 1 tbsp/240g Greek yogurt

1 large egg

1 tbsp orange zest

4 cups plus 2 tbsp/515g all-purpose flour, *plus extra for shaping*

2 tsp ground star anise

1 tsp ground cinnamon

3 tbsp sugar

1 tsp baking soda

½ tsp baking powder

1 tsp salt

5 tbsp/70g unsalted butter, *fridge cold and cut into ½-inch/1½cm cubes*

5¼ oz/150g soft dried figs, *cut into ½-inch/1cm cubes, hard stems removed*

1. Preheat the oven to 400°F. Line a baking sheet with parchment paper.

2. Whisk together the milk, yogurt, egg, and orange zest in a medium bowl and set aside.

3. In a separate large bowl, mix together the flour, spices, sugar, baking soda, baking powder, and salt. Use your hands to rub in the butter until it resembles coarse crumbs similar to large couscous, then stir in the figs. Add the yogurt mixture and stir to gently combine; do not overmix it—you just want the ingredients to come together (it will be very sticky).

4. Using lightly floured hands, transfer the dough to your prepared baking sheet and shape it into a rough, circular mound similar to a loaf of sourdough, about 7 inches/18cm in diameter. Use a sharp knife to gently score an X across the top (don't worry if it's not perfect). Bake for 45 minutes, until nicely browned and a skewer inserted into the center comes out just clean. Transfer to a wire rack to cool, about 45 minutes, before serving.

Make it your own:
- Use other dried fruits and spices (apricot and cardamom would be lovely!).

_____

_____

_____

Yogurt rice with chana dal and curry leaf oil

Prep time: *20 minutes*
Cook time: *1 hour 5 minutes*
Soaking time: *2 hours to overnight*

This take on Indian "curd rice" is all at once creamy, hearty, spicy, and comforting. We added egg yolk to the base, an untraditional twist, but it makes it a little more velvety and rich. Eliminate this if you like.

Serves 4

½ cup/100g chana dal, *soaked in plenty of cold water for at least 2 hours (or overnight)*

1 cup/200g basmati rice, *washed until the water runs clear and drained well*

½ cup plus 1 tbsp/135ml olive oil

1 large egg yolk

⅔ cup/200g Greek yogurt

1 large onion, *finely chopped*

6 garlic cloves, *minced*

1 oz/30g fresh ginger, *peeled and finely grated*

2 small serrano chiles, *1 finely chopped and the other thinly sliced, seeded if you don't like heat*

1 tsp garam masala

3 dried red chiles (*the mild, finger-length variety*)

20 fresh curry leaves (*from 2 sprigs*)

1 tsp black mustard seeds

¼ tsp ground turmeric

salt and black pepper

> **Get ahead:**
> – Make the rice in advance if you like, but thin it out with a little water when reheating.

1. Drain the chana dal, then transfer to a small saucepan with enough water to cover by about 1¼ inches/3cm. Bring to a boil on medium-high heat and simmer for 15–30 minutes, until the dal is cooked but still holds its shape. Timings vary depending on soaking time, so test it at the 15-minute mark (adding more time as needed). Drain in a sieve and run under cold water to stop further cooking.

2. Bring 5½ cups/1.3 liters of water to a boil in a large saucepan. Keep warm on low heat.

3. Put the rice, 2 tablespoons of oil, ¾ cup/180ml of the hot water, and 1¾ teaspoons of salt into a large sauté pan on medium-high heat. Bring to a simmer, stirring often, until most of the water has been absorbed. Continue in this way, adding ¾ cup/180ml of the hot water at a time and stirring often, until you have used up 5 cups/1.2 liters of water and the rice resembles a loose, creamy porridge (it will be overcooked), about 20 minutes.

4. Use the back of a spoon to lightly crush the rice grains— you don't want to mash them completely—then turn the heat down to medium-low.

5. Whisk the egg yolk, yogurt, and 3 tablespoons/50ml of the remaining warm water together in a bowl until smooth. Add this to the rice, stirring often, and cook for 7 minutes—until thickened slightly, but still a loose porridge. Thin out with more warm water if needed; it tends to thicken as it sits.

6. Meanwhile, make the topping. Heat 3 tablespoons of oil in a large frying pan on medium-high heat. Add the onion and cook for 8 minutes, stirring occasionally, until browned. Then add the garlic, ginger, and chopped serrano chile and cook for 4 minutes more. Stir in the chana dal, garam masala, ¼ cup/60ml of water, ¾ teaspoon of salt, and a good grind of pepper, and cook, stirring occasionally, until the chana dal starts to brown in places, about 10 minutes. Transfer to a bowl, and cover to keep warm.

7. Wipe out the pan and return it to medium-high heat. Add the remaining 4 tablespoons of oil and the dried red and sliced serrano chiles and cook for 3 minutes, until starting to soften but not color. Add the curry leaves and cook for another 45 seconds, until translucent. Stir in the mustard seeds and turmeric and remove from the heat.

8. To serve, divide the yogurt rice among four bowls and top with the chana dal mixture. Spoon the curry leaf oil and its solids over the top and serve warm.

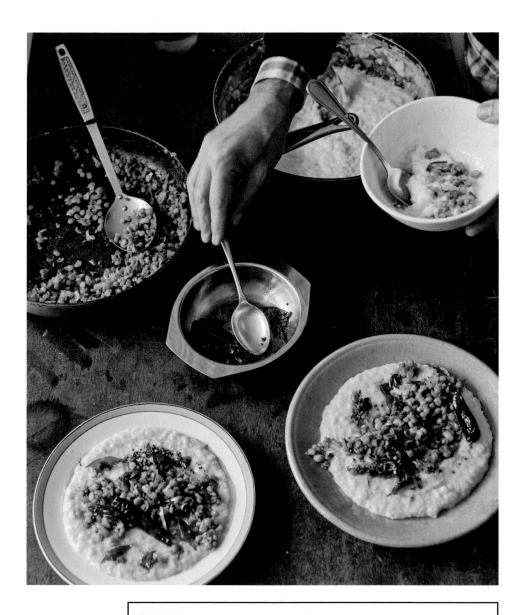

Make it your own:
- Eliminate the chile to make it kid-friendly.
- Swap out the chana dal for other pulses or some roasted vegetables.
- Substitute the curry leaves with fresh basil or cilantro leaves if you like.

Ixta's biang biang noodles

Prep time: *10 minutes*
Cook time: *1 hour*
Resting time: *2 hours 30 minutes +*
Cooling time: *1 hour +*

This recipe is inspired by Xi'an Impression, one of Ixta's favorite restaurants in north London, serving the food of the Shaanxi Province in central China. Determined to learn the art of noodle making, Ixta made this dish during the early days of the first lockdown, showing everyone how to bang bang their biang biang noodles via Instagram. The surge in videos of people making their own were a treat to watch, another way in which food brought the corners of the world together.

It's important to use all-purpose flour with 10–12% protein—any less than 10% and the dough will rip, rather than stretch. You can find the protein amount in the nutrition information on the side of the package. Don't worry too much if the noodles rip at the ends—boil them anyway because they will still taste great with the sauces. The technique takes practice and you'll get better as you make them.

Serves 2

NOODLES

2 cups plus 6 tbsp/300g all-purpose flour *(10–12% protein), sifted*

salt

NUMBING OIL

½ cup plus 2 tbsp/150ml vegetable oil, *plus extra for greasing*

1 shallot, *finely chopped (⅓ cup/60g)*

2 garlic cloves, *finely chopped*

⅓ oz/10g fresh ginger, *peeled and finely grated*

½ small Fresno chile, *finely chopped, seeds and all*

1 whole star anise

1 tbsp red bell pepper flakes, *or 1 tsp Aleppo or Korean gochugaru hot pepper flakes*

1 tsp chile flakes

1½ tsp Szechuan peppercorns, *roughly crushed*

1½ tsp tomato paste

1 tsp black sesame seeds

1 tsp white sesame seeds

1. For the noodles, mix together the flour and ½ teaspoon of salt in a bowl. Very slowly pour in ½ cup plus 2 tablespoons/150ml of water, stirring with a chopstick. It will look a bit dry—don't be tempted to add more water.

2. Transfer to a greased work surface and use your arm muscles to knead the dough for 5 minutes (it will be quite tough) until it comes together into a shaggy ball. Cover with a damp kitchen towel and let rest for 10 minutes.

3. Knead again vigorously for 10 minutes until the dough is very smooth. It should have the texture of Play-Doh. If you poke it, the indentations should remain, not spring back. Cover with a damp kitchen towel and let rest for another 10 minutes.

4. Cut the dough into eight equal pieces, then roll each piece into a sausage and place it on a well-greased baking sheet. Cover well with a damp kitchen towel and let rest at room temperature for 2–3 hours.

5. For the numbing oil, heat 2 tablespoons of oil in a small saucepan on medium-high heat. Add the next eight ingredients and ¼ teaspoon of salt. Turn the heat down to medium and fry very gently for 5 minutes, stirring often, until the shallot is soft. Add the tomato paste and all the sesame seeds and cook for another 2 minutes. Stir in the remaining ½ cup/120ml of oil, then decrease the heat to low and cook gently for 20 minutes. If the oil starts to bubble at all, take it off the heat for 1 minute. Let cool and infuse for at least 1 hour.

6. For the tahini-soy sauce, mix all the ingredients together with 1 tablespoon of water in a bowl until smooth.

7. Prepare two individual bowls with a large spoonful each of the numbing oil and the tahini-soy sauce. Bring a large pot of water to a boil.

TAHINI-SOY SAUCE

¼ cup/60g tahini *(mix very well before using, to combine the solids and oil)*

2 tbsp soy sauce, *plus extra to serve*

1½ tbsp maple syrup

1½ tbsp rice vinegar

TO SERVE

2 green onions, *julienned*

1½ tbsp white sesame seeds, *toasted*

8. When ready, grease your work surface well, then, working with one dough sausage at a time, use a rolling pin to roll it into a rectangle measuring 6½ x 3¼ inches/16 x 8cm. Use a chopstick to indent a line lengthwise across the middle of the rectangle—this will be your ripping line. Continue with all the sausages in the same way. Let rest for 10 minutes.

9. Working with one rectangle at a time, take a shorter end in each hand and start to pull the rectangle slowly and gently until you feel there is no more tension left. Bang the noodle on your work surface about five times, gently stretching the noodle as you go.

10. Using the indent you made earlier, tear the noodle in half lengthwise, but not completely, to form a large closed loop. Drop straight into the pan of boiling water, then immediately continue pulling the remaining noodles and adding them to the water. Cook for 1 minute, or until they float to the top.

11. Drain the noodles well, then divide between your prepared bowls.

12. Use chopsticks to mix the noodles together with the oil and sauce, adding more to taste. Top with the green onions, sesame seeds, and a drizzle of soy sauce.

Make it your own:

– We love these sauces so much, so if you don't have time to make your own noodles we urge you to try them using your choice of store-bought noodles!

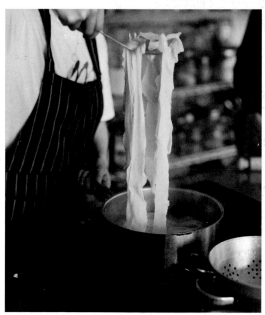

Very giant giant couscous cake

Prep time: *20 minutes*
Cook time: *1 hour 20 minutes*

This very giant cake is very versatile in that you can use other leftover cooked grains or whatever herbs, cheeses, and spices you have on hand. Once you've got all your components at the ready, it's a matter of pressing it into the pan and letting it crisp up before the ultimate cake flip. There are two key ways to ensure cake-flip success here: (1) a nonstick pan; and (2) trust—that it *will* work, that you *can* flip it, that sometimes what is upside down is really right side up. Serve with a big green salad for a complete meal.

Serves 4

1⅔ cups/250g giant/pearl couscous

1⅓ cups/320ml boiling water

10 green onions, *trimmed and left whole (5¼ oz/150g)*

8 tbsp/120ml olive oil

5¼ oz/150g baby spinach

1 tbsp coriander seeds, *toasted and roughly crushed with a mortar and pestle*

1 cup/100g coarsely grated low-moisture mozzarella

½ cup/50g finely grated pecorino, *plus extra to serve*

2 garlic cloves, *minced*

¾ cup/15g basil leaves, *roughly torn, plus a handful of leaves to serve*

¾ cup/220g Greek yogurt

2 large eggs

6 tbsp/50g all-purpose flour

PEPPER SAUCE

2 red bell peppers *(11¼ oz/320g), quartered (9¾ oz/280g)*

1 tomato, *halved (3½ oz/100g)*

4 tbsp/60ml olive oil, *plus extra for drizzling*

2 large heads of garlic, *skin on and top ⅛ trimmed to expose the cloves*

1½ tbsp red wine vinegar

1 tsp maple syrup

salt and black pepper

1. Preheat the oven to 425°F. Put the peppers and tomato on a parchment-lined baking sheet and toss them together with 1 tablespoon of oil, ¼ teaspoon of salt, and a good grind of pepper. Drizzle the garlic heads with a little oil, wrap tightly in foil and place them to one side of the sheet. Roast for 35 minutes, or until the pepper skins are well charred and the garlic has softened.

2. Peel and discard the pepper and tomato skins and put the flesh into a food processor. Squeeze the garlic cloves out of their papery skins and add them to the machine along with the vinegar, maple syrup, ¼ teaspoon of salt, and a good grind of pepper. Blitz for a few seconds, then, with the machine running, slowly drizzle in the remaining 3 tablespoons of oil until the sauce is homogenized and smooth.

3. Meanwhile, put the couscous, ½ teaspoon of salt, and the boiling water into a medium saucepan on medium-high heat. Bring to a simmer, cover with a lid, and turn the heat to medium-low. Cook for 10 minutes, then remove the lid and set aside to cool.

4. Place a large nonstick frying pan on high heat. Toss the green onions in ½ tablespoon of oil and fry in the hot pan for 4 minutes, turning halfway, until softened and lightly charred. Set the green onions aside. Turn the heat down to medium-high, then add another ½ tablespoon of oil and the spinach to the pan. Cook for 90 seconds to wilt, then transfer to a large bowl.

5. Roughly chop the green onions and add two-thirds to the spinach bowl. Add the cooked couscous, crushed coriander seeds, both cheeses, the garlic, basil, yogurt, eggs, flour, ½ teaspoon of salt, and a good grind of pepper and mix together well.

6. Wipe out the frying pan and add 5 tablespoons/75ml of oil on medium-high heat. Once hot, add the couscous mixture, using a spoon to evenly distribute. Turn the heat down to medium and cook for 18 minutes—the edges will start to turn golden and you should be able to loosen the cake from the base. Use a spatula to gently separate the cake from the sides of the pan, running it under the cake to try to loosen it from the bottom. Remove the pan from the heat and, very gently, invert the whole thing onto a large plate.

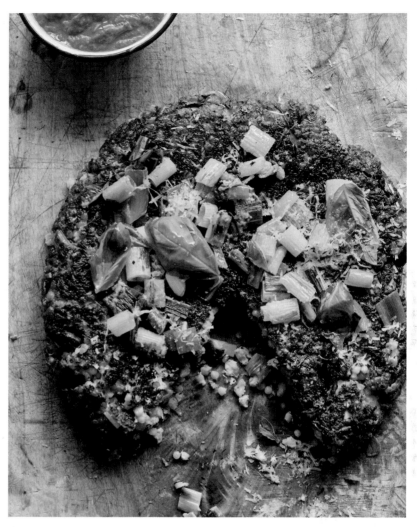

7. Add 1 tablespoon of oil to the pan and slide the cake back into it, crispy side up, to brown the other side. Cook for 8 minutes, on medium heat, before sliding the cake onto a large wooden board or serving platter.

8. In a small bowl, combine the remaining chopped green onions with the extra basil leaves and the last 1 tablespoon of oil. Sprinkle the cake with the extra pecorino and top with the green onion mixture. Serve the pepper sauce in a bowl alongside.

Make it your own:

– Leftover cooked rice or pearl barley, Parmesan and Gruyère, dill or tarragon, toasted cumin or fennel seeds, the options to MIYO are endless.

– Double up on the sauce—it makes a great vegan pasta sauce.

On black limes

More often than not, our cupboards will contain a few obscure ingredients: things you buy for that one recipe, pack away, and then, well, forget about. Black limes are pretty obscure for some; you might have even bought a package for an Ottolenghi recipe asking you to use them. We get it; they can be intimidating if you don't know what to do with them—bitter, astringent, mysterious, to say the least. What even are black limes? Well, they're limes that have been treated with a salt-water solution before being left out to dry in the sun, until completely dehydrated and very dark. Also called Omani limes, loomi aswad, or noomi basra, they're a staple ingredient throughout the Persian Gulf, adding an earthy, bitter depth to the dishes they're used in. If you can't find dried black limes, then you can also use the lighter-colored dried limes, which have more of a greeny-brown hue. Besides their different coloring, the two are pretty much interchangeable. You can use plenty of lime juice and zest as a substitute for dried limes, but in truth, their unique properties are unparalleled. If there's one funky ingredient we want you to pull out of the very back of your cupboards, or maybe even—dare we say—to add to your cupboards, it's a bag of black limes. They last forever, and oh do they pack a punch.

A few black lime hacks:

• Throw them whole into soups and stews, adding a subtle astringent tang. Make sure to poke a few holes in them first—this will help them soften and release their flavor into the liquid they're cooked in.

• Blitz them into a powder to use in rubs and marinades. A coffee or spice grinder is best for this, ensuring the smoothest texture. To help this along, use the palm of your hand to lightly crush the black limes before blitzing.

• Decrease bitterness by removing the seeds, if you wish. Although this isn't really necessary.

• Use the black limes to make a sour tea called chai loomi. Roughly break apart 3–4 limes and remove any seeds. Gently simmer in 1 quart/1 liter of water for 10 minutes, then strain and add fresh mint, a squeeze of lemon juice, and sugar or honey to taste.

• Be sure to purchase black limes that are whole and not ground. You can grind them in a coffee or spice grinder as and when you need to, and they'll keep for much longer.

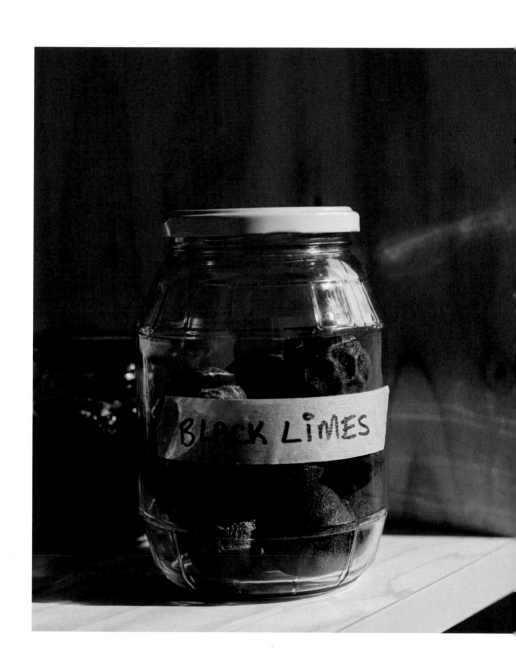

Black lime beef skewers with sumac onions

Prep time: *15 minutes*
Cook time: *25 minutes*
Marinating time: *1 hour to overnight*

Black limes act as both a flavor enhancer and a tenderizer in this marinade, softening the meat but also giving it an edgy tang. This dish is native to Bahrain and is locally called tikka, but is not really tikka as we know it to be. Grilled to order, the tikka comes wrapped up in a little flatbread bundle with raw onion, local arugula (called jarjeer), and lime wedges to squeeze on top. Be sure to source meat with some fat attached—this truly adds to the whole authentic eating experience. We urge you to give this marinade a go, if not with beef then with lamb, chicken, tofu, or meaty mushrooms. Serve this with the roasted potatoes with aïoli (p. 78).

Serves 4

4 sirloin steaks
  (2lb 2 oz/1kg), with some fat attached
5–6 dried black limes
  (p. 50), roughly chopped, then finely ground in a coffee or spice grinder to get 3 tbsp
2 lemons: *finely grate the zest to get 2 tsp and then juice to get 2½ tbsp*
1 tbsp ground cumin
6 garlic cloves, *minced*
3 tbsp olive oil
vegetable oil, *for greasing*
4 naan or pita breads, *store-bought or homemade (p. 23)*
1 tsp Aleppo chile, *or ½ tsp regular chile flakes*
¼ cup/5g parsley leaves
¼ cup/5g mint leaves
salt and black pepper
8 metal skewers, *about 10 inches/25cm long, or wooden skewers soaked in water for 10 minutes*

SUMAC ONIONS
1 red onion, *thinly sliced (1 cup/120g)*
1½ tsp sumac
2¼ tsp apple cider vinegar

1. Place the steaks between two pieces of parchment paper and use a mallet or the bottom of a saucepan to bash them until they're about ¾ inch/2cm thick. Cut the steaks, fat and all, into ¾-inch/2cm cubes and place them in a bowl with the ground black lime, lemon zest and juice, cumin, garlic, 2 tablespoons of olive oil, 1½ teaspoons of salt, and a good grind of pepper. Let marinate for at least 1 hour, or refrigerate overnight.

2. For the sumac onions, mix the onion, sumac, vinegar, and ⅛ teaspoon of salt together and allow to soften for at least 30 minutes.

3. Thread the beef on to the skewers, packing the cubes closely together.

4. Heat a well-greased grill pan on high heat. Once smoking and very hot, cook the skewers in batches for about 3–4 minutes per batch, until charred but not overcooked, turning as necessary. Transfer to a baking sheet and cover with foil to keep warm.

5. Warm the bread in the hot grill pan for about 30 seconds on each side.

6. Lay the bread out on a platter and top with the skewers, brushing them with the remaining 1 tablespoon of olive oil and sprinkling with the chile. Nestle the herbs to one side and serve with the sumac onions.

Sesame-crusted feta
with black lime honey syrup

Prep time: *15 minutes*
Cook time: *30 minutes*
Chilling time: *30 minutes*
to overnight

"Everything is betta with feta," says Tara, voted the number one feta fan of all time, and, to be fair, she might be right. We try really hard not to show cheese favoritism (cheesism), but we'd be lying if we didn't admit that feta makes a prominent appearance in the OTK fridge, its salty, tangy properties lending it well to multiple preparations.

This dish is a little bit sweet, a lotta bit salty, a tiny bit bitter, and a whole bit crispy. It's exactly what you'd serve for brunch (with bacon, if you like) and not much else, as it really is quite rich.

Serves 8

2 blocks of Greek feta
(*12¾ oz/360g), each cut into 4 triangles (8 triangles in total)*

¼ cup/35g rice flour
(*or all-purpose flour if gluten-free flour not needed)*

1 large egg, *well beaten*

⅔ cup/100g mixed black and white sesame seeds, *lightly toasted*

2 tbsp olive oil

½ tbsp lemon thyme leaves, *or regular thyme leaves*

SYRUP

⅓ cup/120g honey

1 tsp ground black lime
(*p. 50) (optional)*

3 lemons: *1 juiced to get 1 tbsp and the other 2 left whole*

Get ahead:
– Coat the feta the night before, cover well, and keep refrigerated.

---

1. Line a shallow baking dish (or baking sheet with a slight lip), about 12 x 8 inches/30 x 20cm in size, with parchment paper.

2. Pat dry the feta pieces, then dip each piece in the flour, gently shaking off the excess. Coat in the egg, followed by the sesame seeds, making sure the feta pieces are completely coated. Transfer each piece to the prepared dish and refrigerate for at least 30 minutes, or up to overnight.

3. Preheat the oven to 450°F. Drizzle the coated feta pieces with the oil and bake from cold, for 18 minutes, very gently flipping the pieces over halfway, or until golden and warmed through.

4. While the feta is baking, put the honey and black lime, if using, into a small saucepan on medium-high heat. Once it starts to bubble, turn the heat to medium and cook, stirring occasionally, until it turns a deep amber caramel, about 6–7 minutes. Take off the heat and stir in the lemon juice. Set aside to cool for 5 minutes.

5. Use a small, sharp knife to peel and segment the remaining two lemons and stir the segments into the cooled honey mixture.

6. When ready, pour the syrup directly over the feta in the baking dish, sprinkle with the thyme, and serve at once, straight from the dish.

Make it your own:
– Leave out the black lime if you can't find any—this dish is just as special without it.
– Swap out the feta for halloumi cheese instead.

_____

_____

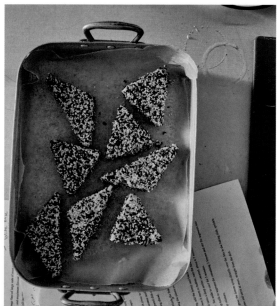

Tabbouleh fritters with quick chile sauce

Prep time: *25 minutes*
Cook time: *45 minutes*

You can choose to eat these as they are or, for the ultimate veggie pita, make the homemade pitas on p. 23, open them up into a pocket, and stuff them with these fritters, the chile sauce, tahini sauce (p. 27), and some raw veggies. Make sure you have some napkins handy!

Makes 8 fritters to serve 4

½ cup/70g bulgur wheat

7 oz/200g baby spinach

2½ cups/50g parsley, *roughly chopped*

1 cup/20g mint leaves

½ red onion, *roughly chopped (⅓ cup/60g)*

1 garlic clove, *roughly chopped*

1 tsp ground allspice

1 tsp ground cinnamon

1 tbsp finely grated lemon zest

5 tbsp/75ml olive oil

3 large eggs

salt and black pepper

QUICK CHILE SAUCE

3 tbsp olive oil

2 garlic cloves, *roughly chopped*

½ yellow onion, *roughly chopped (½ cup/75g)*

4 tsp tomato paste

2 small Fresno chiles, *roughly chopped, seeds and all (2 tbsp/20g)*

2 vine tomatoes, *roughly chopped, seeds and all (mounded 1 cup/200g)*

1½ tbsp apple cider vinegar

1. Put the bulgur wheat into a small saucepan with 5 table-spoons/75ml of water and ¼ teaspoon of salt. Bring to a boil, cover with a lid, then remove from the heat. Let sit and steam gently, covered, for 10 minutes, then fluff up with a fork. Allow to cool.

2. Meanwhile, make the chile sauce by heating the oil in a small frying pan on medium-high heat. Add the garlic and onion and cook for 5 minutes, stirring occasionally, until softened and lightly colored. Add the tomato paste and cook for 1 minute more, stirring continuously, then add the chiles and remove from the heat. Let cool for 5 minutes, then transfer to a food processor and pulse a few times until finely chopped. Add the tomatoes, vinegar, and the ½ teaspoon of salt and pulse to a semi-smooth purée. Transfer to a bowl.

3. Blanch the spinach in plenty of boiling water for just 20 seconds. Drain, running under cold water, then squeeze out as much liquid as possible. You need 3¼ oz/90g.

4. Put the cooled bulgur wheat, blanched spinach, herbs, red onion, garlic, spices, lemon zest, 1 tablespoon of oil, ¾ teaspoon of salt, and a good grind of pepper into the food processor and pulse a couple of times, until finely chopped. Add the eggs and pulse a few times more, until just combined. Transfer the batter to a bowl.

5. Heat the remaining 4 table-spoons of oil in a large sauté pan on medium-high heat. Add large spoonfuls of the batter to the pan and gently shape to form 2½–3-inch/6–7cm patties about ¾ inch/2cm thick. Fry 3–4 at a time, about 2–3 minutes per side, to make eight in total. Turn down the heat if they get too dark.

6. Serve the fritters warm, with the quick chile sauce alongside.

56

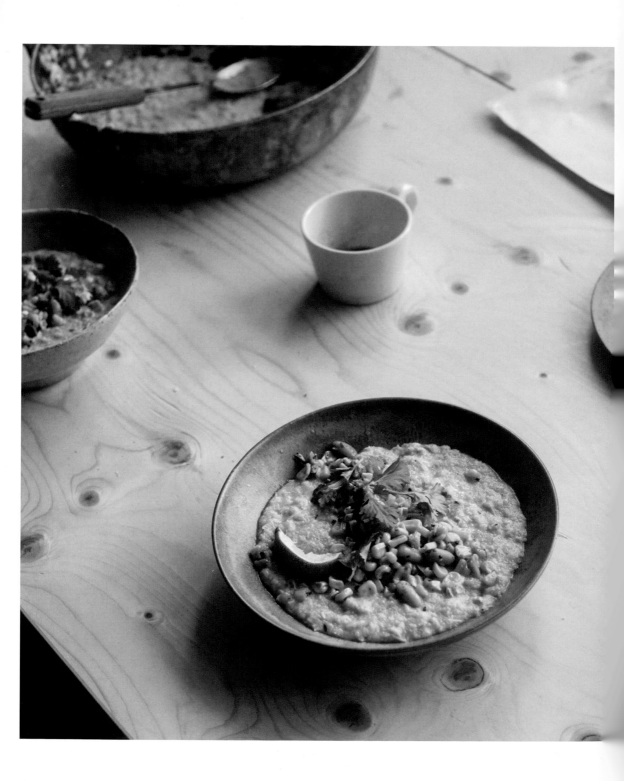

Spiced semolina with corn, peanuts, and cilantro

Prep time: *15 minutes*
Cook time: *20 minutes*

Semolina is, more often than not, overlooked in favor of its similar-natured cousin polenta. They can both be used for the same purposes really, making wonderful desserts and breads or eaten warm as a side. That being said, they are distant cousins (twice removed), and therefore still have their own individual attributes—with semolina being slightly creamier, especially when cooked in this porridge-like way. Make sure to source the medium to coarse semolina and not the super-fine one. Serve as a brunch, or for dinner with some broiled shrimp or tofu.

Serves 4

3 tbsp olive oil

½ tsp black mustard seeds

1 tsp cumin seeds

½ tsp ground cinnamon

2 whole cloves

2 cups/350g corn kernels *(from 2–3 cobs), or the frozen equivalent, defrosted*

1 small serrano chile, *finely chopped, seeds and all (1 tbsp/10g)*

¼ tsp asafoetida

½ cup/60g roasted and salted peanuts

2–3 limes: *1–2 juiced to get 2 tbsp, and the other cut into 4 wedges to serve*

¾ oz/20g fresh ginger, *peeled and finely grated*

2 garlic cloves, *minced*

¾ cup plus 2 tbsp/200ml full-fat coconut milk, *plus 2 tbsp extra to serve*

¼ tsp ground turmeric

½ cup/75g medium to coarse semolina

¼ cup/5g cilantro leaves, *with some stem attached*

salt

1. Put 1 tablespoon of oil into a large sauté pan on medium-high heat. Add the mustard seeds, cumin seeds, cinnamon, and cloves and fry for about 30–60 seconds, until the seeds start to pop. Add the corn, half the chile, the asafoetida, and ½ teaspoon of salt and cook for 3 minutes, stirring occasionally, until fragrant. Add the peanuts and cook for 3 minutes more, or until the mixture takes on some color. Off the heat, add the lime juice and discard the cloves.

2. Transfer half the corn mixture to a food processor and blitz to a coarse paste. Set both corn mixtures aside, separately, until ready to use.

3. Put the remaining 2 tablespoons of oil into a medium saucepan and put on medium-high heat. Add the ginger, garlic, and remaining serrano chile and fry for 90 seconds, until fragrant. Add 1⅔ cups/400ml of water, the coconut milk, turmeric, and ¾ teaspoon of salt and bring to a boil.

4. Once boiling, lower the heat to medium and slowly add the semolina, whisking constantly to avoid any lumps. Continue to whisk for 3 minutes, until the consistency is that of thin porridge. Add the blitzed corn mixture and cook for 1 minute, stirring constantly, until thickened slightly.

5. Divide the porridge among four bowls and drizzle with the extra coconut milk. Mix the cilantro leaves into the sautéed corn mix and spoon this over the top. Serve warm with a lime wedge.

Make it your own:

– Asafoetida is a pungent onion-garlicky spice used a lot in southern Indian cooking. Leave it out if you can't find any; it's still just as good without.

– Play with the nuts and spices!

– Use instant polenta instead of semolina, adjusting liquid levels accordingly.

Veg

Your

Box

Your veg box

There's no secret that the OTK crew stands faithfully behind Yotam's love affair with vegetables. We have an all-inclusive, every-vegetable-counts policy, which sometimes means that narrowing the options down can prove difficult. We therefore stuck to the most accessible vegetables as we ate and tested our way through the seasons, while keeping the make-it-your-own options as expansive as possible. Big bundles of herbs and plenty of leafy greens, a few eggplants, a bag of onions, and a very large butternut squash. If these were the contents of your veg box or CSA share, what would you do with it all?

Focusing on the culinary positives of recent times, many of us have upped the hours we spend in the kitchen cooking for ourselves and our households. We've also spent some time digging through veg box (or CSA) deliveries, or rummaging through the season's finds at our local farmers' market or supermarket. This has sometimes meant less choice to play with on the one hand, but also way more perishable goods to reckon with on the other.

In this chapter, we aim to help you navigate through your vegetable finds while also keeping a few things in mind. The first is frugality—the need to use up what's on hand: a few flimsy-looking eggplants soon become burnt eggplant, tomato, and tahini (p. 83). The second is creativity, or more likely an aversion to monotony, turning sweet potato flesh into shakshuka and saving the skins for a crispy snack (p. 84). The last is mindfulness, of perfectly imperfect produce, the "whats" of what's in season and the "hows" of how best to use them—using funky-looking tomatoes in the not-your-average tomato salad (p. 67). All the while we invite you to substitute and swap out, finding innovative solutions to leave your own mark on these dishes.

This is a journey through our veg boxes, embracing the multitude of ways in which we treat our vegetables—smooshed, grated, broiled, roasted—and the various ways in which we serve them—with eggs, on warm yogurt, spooned onto bread, etc.—helping you answer the question "What will I do with my veg box?"

Green herb bagna cauda

Prep time: *35 minutes*
Cook time: *45 minutes*

This dip is loosely based on bagna càuda, an Italian dish made from anchovies, garlic, and olive oil. Here we add earthy cooked herbs and vibrant fresh ones—increasing the dip's savory intensity and making it perfect for crudités. We like using up all the bits in our seasonal veg box as little vehicles to scoop and eat with, but you could just as easily serve this with crackers or crusty bread.

Serves 6, as a snack

⅔ cup plus 3 tbsp/200ml
  olive oil, *plus extra
  for drizzling*

2 onions, *halved and thinly
  sliced (10½ oz/300g)*

3½ cups/70g parsley,
  roughly chopped

3½ cups/70g cilantro,
  roughly chopped

2½ cups/50g dill, *roughly
  chopped*

8 green onions, *finely
  sliced (1 cup/80g)*

½ tsp ground turmeric

2 tsp cumin seeds, *roughly
  crushed with a mortar and
  pestle*

15 garlic cloves, *peeled*

**12 anchovies packed
  in olive oil,** *drained
  (1½ oz/40g)*

5 tbsp/75ml lemon juice

1 cup/20g mint leaves

salt and black pepper

ANY-STYLE CRUDITÉS

**1 Italian radicchio
  trevisano** *(or red endive),
  leaves separated*

**5¼ oz/150g baby
  carrots,** *peeled and
  halved lengthwise*

**3½ oz/100g sugar snap
  peas,** *stringy bits removed*

**5¼ oz/150g rainbow or
  breakfast radishes,** *halved*

1. Put 3 tablespoons of oil into a large sauté pan on medium-high heat. Once hot, cook the onions for 12–15 minutes, stirring, until softened and browned. Transfer half the onions and oil to a bowl and return the pan to medium heat. Add 2½ cups/50g each of the parsley and cilantro, 2 cups/40g of the dill, and all the green onions, and cook, stirring often, for 15 minutes, or until deeply green and fragrant, but not browned. Add the turmeric and cumin and cook for 3 minutes more. Set aside to cool.

2. Meanwhile, put the garlic and the remaining ⅔ cup/155ml of oil into a small saucepan, for which you have a lid. Place on medium-low heat, covered, and cook for 10 minutes, stirring once, until the garlic has started to soften. Add the anchovies, replace the lid, and cook for 10 minutes more. Remove from the heat and let cool.

3. Put the herb mixture and garlic mixture into a food processor along with the lemon juice, mint, the remaining parsley, cilantro, and dill, ¼ teaspoon of salt, and a good grind of pepper, and blitz until smooth.

4. Transfer to a bowl and top with the reserved browned onions, stirring them in a little. Place on a board and arrange the crudités all around. Lastly, drizzle the crudités with a little oil and season them lightly with salt and pepper.

Make it your own:

- Use up whatever mixture of soft herbs and green onions you have, so long as it comes to 9⅓ oz/265g worth of herbage.
- Veganize it: swap out the anchovies for 2 tablespoons of capers.

_____

_____

Not-your-average tomato salad

Prep time: *20 minutes*
Cook time: *40 minutes*

The flavorful dressing is what makes this salad so unique, thanks to the infused ginger and garlic oil that certifiably takes your tomato salad game to beyond average. Use whatever mixture of tomatoes you can find, making sure they're wonderfully ripe and in season. Make this salad vegan by swapping out the fish sauce for light soy sauce, adjusting salt levels accordingly.

Serves 4, as a side

5 garlic cloves, *thinly sliced*

1¼ oz/35g fresh ginger, *peeled and julienned*

½ cup plus 1 tbsp/135ml olive oil

3–4 limes: *finely grate the zest to get 1 tbsp and then juice to get 3 tbsp*

2 tbsp fish sauce

½ cup/10g cilantro leaves, *roughly chopped*

1 lb 2 oz/500g heirloom tomatoes, *cored and cut into ½-inch/1½cm-thick slices*

10½ oz/300g mixed cherry tomatoes *(red/yellow/ orange), halved lengthwise*

½ red onion, *cut into thin rounds (2¼ oz/60g)*

flaked sea salt and black pepper

1. Put the garlic, ginger, oil, and ½ teaspoon of flaked sea salt into a small sauté pan and place it on medium-low heat. Cook gently for 25 minutes, swirling the pan occasionally, until the solids are lightly golden. Strain the oil through a sieve set over a bowl and set aside to cool for 10 minutes. Transfer the solids to a plate lined with paper towels to crisp up further.

2. Use a fork to whisk the lime zest, lime juice, fish sauce, and cilantro into the cooled ginger-garlic oil until combined.

3. Gently toss all the tomatoes together with 1 teaspoon of flaked sea salt and a generous grind of pepper. Arrange the tomatoes and red onion on a large platter and spoon the dressing over the top, followed by the crispy ginger and garlic. Serve right away.

Smooshed carrots with cilantro-pistachio pesto and pickled onions

Prep time: *25 minutes*
Cook time: *1 hour 15 minutes*

Think big, bold colors and flavors: this dish is a good way to dress up the humble carrot in its most fantastic party attire. Serve this as part of a mezze spread or as a side to your protein of choice.

Serves 4, as a side or part of a mezze spread

½ **small red onion,** *finely chopped (⅓ cup/50g)*

2 **tbsp lime juice**

2½ **lb/1.2kg carrots,** *peeled and cut crosswise into 1¼–1½-inch/3–4cm chunks*

9 **tbsp/135ml olive oil**

¾ **tsp ground turmeric**

7 **garlic cloves,** *peeled, 6 left whole and 1 minced*

2 **tsp coriander seeds,** *roughly crushed with a mortar and pestle*

2 **tsp cumin seeds,** *roughly crushed with a mortar and pestle*

½ **tsp chile flakes**

1½ **tbsp maple or agave syrup**

1 **cup/20g cilantro,** *roughly chopped*

3 **green onions,** *thinly sliced (⅓ cup/30g)*

⅓ **cup/40g pistachios,** *very lightly toasted and roughly chopped*

¼ **cup/60g Greek yogurt**

salt and black pepper

1. Preheat the oven to 400°F.

2. In a small bowl, mix together the onion, 1 tablespoon of lime juice, and a pinch of salt and set aside to pickle.

3. Put the carrots, 4 tablespoons of oil, the turmeric, ¾ cup plus 2 tablespoons/200ml of water, ½ teaspoon salt, and a good grind of pepper into a medium baking dish and mix everything together. Roast for 25 minutes, then add the whole garlic cloves and the spices and return to the oven for another 20 minutes, or until the carrots are cooked through. Turn the oven temperature up to 450°F, drizzle the carrots all over with the maple or agave syrup, and return to the oven for 10 minutes, or until the carrots have taken on a little color. Let cool for about 5 minutes, then use a fork or potato masher to smoosh everything together into a coarse mash (you don't want it super smooth).

4. Meanwhile, make the pesto. Put the cilantro, green onions, pistachios, 3 tablespoons of oil, minced garlic, ¼ teaspoon of salt, and a good grind of pepper into a food processor and blitz to a coarse paste. Transfer the pesto to a medium bowl and stir in the last 2 tablespoons of oil.

5. Make the lime yogurt by combining the yogurt with the remaining 1 tablespoon of lime juice in a small bowl.

6. Spread the carrot mash out on a large plate and dot with spoonfuls of the yogurt, followed by about two-thirds of the pesto (serving the remainder alongside). Finally, top with the pickled onion and serve warm or at room temperature.

Make it your own:
- No carrots? No problem. Use sweet potatoes or butternut squash instead.
- Swap out cilantro for parsley, and pistachios for pine nuts or almonds.
- Veganize it: leave out the lime yogurt, or use a non-dairy yogurt instead.

(All the) herb dumplings with caramelized onions

Prep time: *25 minutes*
Cook time: *1 hour 30 minutes*

We love the abundance of herbs at play here, which lends a deep earthiness to these dumplings. Cooking down the herbs in this way is a technique quite distinct to the Middle East, where herbs are used liberally as a base for soups and stews, adding bulk and heft, rather than as a finishing touch. When cooking herbs, patience is key: cook them on moderate heat and stir often; they'll start to lose their vibrancy and become wonderfully fragrant and deeply green, adding a whole other dimension to your dishes. They're only cooked here for 20 minutes or so, but could go for much longer, intensifying with time. Feel free to play around with the herbs if you wish, using more or less of your choosing, depending on what you have. The real star of the dish, though, is the onions, cooked low and slow with saffron and cardamom and a generous amount of butter. Serve this alongside a summery salad and some crusty bread, for a complete meal.

Serves 4, as a starter or side

2 lb 2 oz/1kg onions *(about 5–6), halved and sliced ¼ inch/½cm thick*

10 cardamom pods, *roughly bashed open with a mortar and pestle*

¼ cup/60ml olive oil

8 tbsp/110g unsalted butter, *at room temperature*

4 garlic cloves, *minced*

5 cups/100g cilantro, *roughly chopped*

5 cups/100g parsley, *roughly chopped*

3½ cups/70g dill, *roughly chopped*

1½ cups/30g tarragon leaves, *roughly chopped*

10 green onions, *thinly sliced (1½ cups/105g)*

1½ tsp cumin seeds, *roughly crushed with a mortar and pestle*

¾ tsp ground turmeric

3 tbsp whole-milk ricotta

3½ oz/100g Greek feta, *roughly crumbled*

½ cup/60g finely grated Parmesan

1 large egg

½ cup plus 1 tbsp/70g all-purpose flour

⅓ tsp saffron threads, *roughly crumbled*

2 tbsp lemon juice

salt and black pepper

1. Preheat the oven to 400°F.

2. Put the onions, cardamom, half the oil, 3 tablespoons/40g of butter, and 1 teaspoon of salt into a medium baking dish and mix together to combine. Bake for 60–70 minutes, stirring 4–5 times during, until softened and nicely caramelized.

3. Meanwhile, heat the remaining 2 tablespoons of oil in a large, nonstick sauté pan on medium heat. Add the herbs and green onions and cook, stirring often, for about 10 minutes. Add the cumin and turmeric and cook for 10 minutes more, or until the herbs are deeply green and fragrant. Set aside to cool.

4. Beat together the ricotta, feta, 6 tablespoons/50g of the Parmesan, the egg, 1 teaspoon of salt, and plenty of pepper in a large bowl. Add the flour and the cooled herb mixture and mix well. Refrigerate to set, about 20–40 minutes. Use your hands to

roll into 12 compact dumplings, 1½–1¾ oz/45–50g each.

5. Bring a large pot of water to a boil, then turn the heat down to a bare simmer on medium heat. Drop in the dumplings and cook for 10–12 minutes, or until they rise to the surface and have cooked through the center. Use a slotted spoon to gently transfer the dumplings to a baking sheet lined with paper towels, to dry.

6. When the onions are ready and hot from the oven, add the remaining 5 tablespoons/70g of butter, the saffron, and the lemon juice and mix everything to combine. Turn the oven temperature up to 425°F.

7. Top the onions with the dumplings, slightly spaced apart, then sprinkle all over with the remaining 2 tablespoons/10g of Parmesan. Return to the oven for 8–10 minutes, or until everything is bubbling and warmed through.

Make it your own:

– Use any mixture of herbs you have on hand, using more or less of what you like.
– You can swap out the herbs for spinach, cooking it just enough to release any water. Make sure you then wring it well.

Spiced mashed eggplant and peas

Prep time: *25 minutes*
Cook time: *40 minutes*

More often than not, staff food at the Ottolenghi delis uses up leftover roasted vegetables, mixed with some of our abundance of spices to make different types of curries. Roasted eggplants are therefore in regular rotation on the staff food menu, the mighty eggplant a core part of what makes Ottolenghi, well . . . Ottolenghi. This is a very loose take on baingan bharta, an Indian mashed eggplant dish. On quieter days, a few treasured staff have whipped up some homemade roti to serve alongside, but more often than not we'll have this with plain rice.

Serves 4

3 eggplants *(1 lb 10 oz/ 750g), stems discarded and flesh roughly cut into 1¼–1½-inch/3–4cm cubes*

8 tbsp/120ml olive oil

5¼ oz/150g cherry tomatoes

1 red onion, *thinly sliced (4¼ oz/120g)*

6 garlic cloves, *minced*

1 oz/30g fresh ginger, *peeled and finely chopped*

1 small serrano chile, *finely chopped, seeds and all*

1 tsp black mustard seeds

1 tsp ground turmeric

1 tsp garam masala

1 tsp ground cumin

5¼ oz/150g canned whole, peeled tomatoes *(about ⅔ of a can), roughly crushed by hand*

1 cup/20g cilantro, *roughly chopped*

2 tbsp lemon juice

1⅓ cups/200g frozen peas, *defrosted*

3 green onions, *finely sliced at an angle (⅓ cup/30g)*

2 tbsp Greek yogurt

salt and black pepper

1. Preheat the oven to 450°F. Toss the eggplant pieces together with 4 tablespoons of oil, ¾ teaspoon of salt, and a good grind of pepper on a large, parchment-lined baking sheet, and roast for 20 minutes. Add the cherry tomatoes, giving everything a stir, and return to the oven for another 10 minutes, until the tomatoes have blistered and the eggplant is deeply golden.

2. Meanwhile, make the sauce. Put 2 tablespoons of oil into a large sauté pan on medium-high heat. Add the onion and cook for 7 minutes, stirring occasionally, until nicely browned. Add the garlic, ginger, and chile and cook for 2 minutes more, until fragrant, then add the spices and cook for 30 seconds. Add the canned tomatoes, 1¼ cups/300ml of water, ½ teaspoon of salt, and plenty of pepper, and bring to a simmer. Lower the heat to medium and cook for 15 minutes, stirring every now and then, until thick and rich. Stir in two-thirds of the cilantro, 1 tablespoon of lemon juice, and the roasted vegetables and use a fork to roughly mash every together.

3. In a separate bowl, toss together the peas, the remaining cilantro, the green onions, 1 tablespoon of oil, ¼ teaspoon of salt, and a good grind of pepper.

4. In a small bowl, combine the yogurt with a pinch of salt and the remaining 1 tablespoon of lemon juice.

5. Transfer the mashed eggplant to a serving plate and top with the pea mixture. Drizzle all over with the yogurt and the remaining 1 tablespoon of oil, and serve warm.

Make it your own:

- Veganize it: drizzle with a little coconut milk in place of the yogurt.
- Play with the spices. It's okay if you don't have them all! Use more or less of what you do have.

_____

_____

Charred zucchini with warm yogurt and saffron butter

Prep time: *10 minutes*
Cook time: *30 minutes*

This recipe is inspired by kousa b'laban, a Levantine dish of stuffed baby zucchini cooked in yogurt. In this simplified version the yogurt sauce and broiled zucchini are cooked separately, then served with a quick saffron butter to spoon on top.

There's a bit of an art to cooking yogurt without having it curdle; stabilizers such as cornstarch and egg yolk tend to do the trick, as does cooking the yogurt on moderate heat, stirring continuously and gently warming through without boiling. The result: a silky-smooth and tangy sauce, great for these zucchini but also with other grilled veggies, fatty meats, or even as a sauce for pasta.

Serves 2–4

2 tbsp unsalted butter
¼ tsp saffron threads, *roughly crumbled*
4 small, pale green or regular zucchini, *tops trimmed slightly and zucchini halved lengthwise (1 lb 5 oz/600g)*
2½ tbsp olive oil
1 tsp cornstarch
1 cup plus 1 tbsp/300g Greek yogurt
2 garlic cloves, *minced*
½ tsp dried mint
¾ tsp coriander seeds, *toasted and roughly crushed with a mortar and pestle*
1½ tbsp mint leaves
½ lemon
salt and black pepper

1. Preheat the oven broiler to high.

2. Put the butter and saffron into a small saucepan on medium heat. When the butter has melted, set aside to infuse.

3. Place the zucchini on a parchment-lined baking sheet and toss with 2 tablespoons of oil, ⅓ teaspoon of salt, and a good grind of pepper. Arrange them cut side up and broil for 15–20 minutes, until nicely charred and softened.

4. Toward the last 10 minutes of broiling time, make the sauce. In a large bowl, whisk together the cornstarch and 3 tablespoons of water until smooth, then add the yogurt, garlic, dried mint, the remaining ½ tablespoon of oil, and ½ teaspoon of salt. Whisk to combine, then transfer to a large, nonstick sauté pan on medium heat. Cook, stirring continuously, for about 10 minutes, or until thickened slightly and warmed through. Do not let the sauce boil, or it will split.

5. Transfer the warm yogurt sauce to a plate with a lip and top with the zucchini, broiled side up. Spoon the saffron butter over the top, then sprinkle with the coriander seeds and mint leaves. Squeeze the lemon half over everything and serve right away.

> *Make it your own:*
> – No saffron? Use a pinch of turmeric instead.
> _____
> _____

Roasted pepper salad
with cucumber and herbs

Prep time: *20 minutes*
Cook time: *40 minutes*

This is a take on Tunisian mechouia, a grilled vegetable salad to which we've added fresh cucumber and herbs. You can eat this warm or at room temperature, as a starter or side. It also works well spooned into a sandwich, with plenty of peppery arugula and a good glug of olive oil. A special shout-out to Paula Wolfert and her beautifully informative book *The Food of Morocco*, which makes a sneaky appearance in this photo.

Serves 4, as a starter or side

4 green bell peppers
(1 lb 5 oz/600g), stems and seeds discarded, and flesh cut into roughly 1½-inch/4cm pieces

2 red bell peppers
(10½ oz/300g), stems and seeds discarded, and flesh cut into roughly 1½-inch/4cm pieces

4 vine tomatoes
(14 oz/400g), each cut into quarters

2 small red onions
(7 oz/200g), cut into roughly 1¼-inch/3cm pieces

1 small serrano chile, *stem removed and left whole (⅓ oz/10g)*

6 large garlic cloves, *peeled*

6 tbsp/90ml olive oil

1½ tbsp lemon juice

½ cup/10g parsley, *roughly chopped*

½ cup/ 10g cilantro, *roughly chopped*

1 English cucumber,
peeled, deseeded, and cut into ½-inch/1cm cubes (2¼ cups/330g)

¾ tsp Urfa chile, *or regular chile flakes*

salt and black pepper

1. Preheat the oven to 475°F.

2. In a large bowl, toss together both peppers, the tomatoes, onions, chile, garlic, 4 tablespoons of oil, ¾ teaspoon of salt, and a good grind of pepper. Spread out on two large, parchment-lined baking sheets and roast for about 30 minutes, stirring once or twice during cooking, until the vegetables are softened and charred.

3. Once cool enough to handle, coarsely chop the vegetables into a chunky mash and transfer to a bowl along with the lemon juice, herbs, ½ teaspoon of salt, and a good grind of pepper.

4. In a separate, medium bowl, toss the cucumber with the remaining 2 tablespoons of oil, ¼ teaspoon of salt, and a grind of pepper.

5. Spread the roasted pepper mixture on a plate. Spoon the cucumber over the top and sprinkle with the chile.

Make it your own:

– Keep this kid-friendly by eliminating or decreasing the amount of chile.
– Swap out the cucumber for another crunchy veg, such as celery or kohlrabi.

_____

_____

_____

Roasted potatoes with aïoli and buttered pine nuts

Prep time: *10 minutes*
Cook time: *50 minutes*

Kebab shop fries with mayo are the inspiration for this dish, although this version is a little more involved. There's a generous sauce-to-potato ratio here, which is kind of naughty, but also what you really, truly want. This goes really well with the black lime beef skewers (p. 52).

Serves 4, as a side

1 lb 10 oz/750g baby new
   potatoes, *skin on and*
   halved lengthwise
2 tbsp olive oil
¼ cup/5g parsley, *roughly*
   chopped
salt and black pepper

AÏOLI
2 large garlic cloves,
   minced
1 tsp Dijon mustard
1 large egg
1 large egg yolk
7 tbsp/100ml olive oil
7 tbsp/100ml sunflower oil
1 tbsp lemon juice
¼ cup/75g Greek yogurt

BUTTERED PINE NUTS
2 tbsp unsalted butter
3 tbsp pine nuts
¼ tsp smoked paprika

1. Preheat the oven to 450°F.

2. Put the potatoes and 2 teaspoons of salt into a medium saucepan and pour in plenty of cold water, to cover by about 1½ inches/4cm. Place on medium-high heat, bring to a boil, then simmer for 6 minutes, or until the potatoes are almost cooked through but still with a bite. Drain them in a sieve and pat dry, then transfer to a parchment-lined baking sheet and toss with the oil, ⅓ teaspoon of salt, and a good grind of pepper. Roast, stirring once or twice, for 35 minutes, or until deeply golden. Stir in the parsley.

3. Meanwhile, make the aïoli by putting the garlic, mustard, egg, yolk, and ¼ teaspoon of salt into the bowl of a food processor and blitzing until combined, about 10 seconds. With the machine still running, add both oils in a very slow and steady stream, until you have a loose, mayonnaise-like consistency. Transfer to a bowl, stir in the lemon juice and yogurt, and set aside (or refrigerate) until needed.

4. Put the butter into a small sauté pan on medium heat. Once melted, add the pine nuts and cook until golden, about 3–4 minutes. Stir in the paprika, then remove from the heat and transfer to a bowl.

5. Spread the aïoli out on a round shallow platter. Top with the warm potatoes and spoon the buttered pine nuts over the top.

Make it your own:
- If you can't find baby new potatoes, just use regular new potatoes and cut them into ½-inch/1½cm slices.
- Play with the nuts. Roughly chopped blanched almonds or hazelnuts would be great here!
- Veganize it: use chickpea mayo (p. 32) instead, and olive oil in place of the butter.

Summer zucchini with tomatoes and ricotta

Prep time: *25 minutes*
Cook time: *25 minutes*

There are no tricks here, no clever Ottolenghi twists or obscure ingredients. This is a fairly simple dish that tastes like an Italian summer holiday, and is a nod to the old adage that less is sometimes more. Use the best in-season produce you can find and eat it as is—it really is that good.

Serves 4, as a starter or side

3½ tbsp olive oil

5 garlic cloves, *finely sliced on a mandolin or by hand*

1 lb 10 oz/750g mixed green and yellow zucchini, *quartered lengthwise, then cut into ¾-inch/2cm pieces*

10 sprigs/5g oregano

3 strips lemon peel

½ cup/10g basil leaves

½ cup/120g whole-milk ricotta

TOMATO SALSA

4 very ripe plum tomatoes, *finely chopped (2¼ cups/400g)*

2 tsp finely chopped oregano leaves

1 tsp lemon juice

2 tbsp olive oil

1 small garlic clove, *minced*

salt and black pepper

1. Mix all the ingredients for the tomato salsa together with ¼ teaspoon of salt and a good grind of pepper. Set aside.

2. Place a large, nonstick sauté pan on medium-high heat with 2 tablespoons of oil and the garlic. Gently fry for 3 minutes, stirring often, until the garlic is soft and aromatic. You don't want it to brown at all, so turn the heat down if necessary.

3. Add the zucchini, oregano, lemon peel, ¼ cup/5g of basil leaves, and ¾ teaspoon of salt. Cook for 15 minutes, stirring every now and then, until the zucchini are very soft, but still mostly holding their shape. You don't want the zucchini to brown, so turn the heat down if they do.

4. Remove the cooked basil, oregano, and lemon peel from the zucchini and discard. Transfer the zucchini to a large plate with a lip. Spoon the tomato salsa evenly over the zucchini, then top with spoonfuls of the ricotta. Drizzle with the remaining 1½ tablespoons of oil and season with a pinch of salt. Finish with the remaining ¼ cup/5g of basil leaves and serve.

Make it your own:
- Swap out the ricotta for torn buffalo mozzarella.
- Veganize it: this tastes just as delicious without the cheese!

_____

_____

_____

Burnt eggplant, tomato, and tahini

Prep time: *20 minutes*
Cook time: *1 hour
10 minutes*

This dish was born out of some leftover tomato pasta sauce, as well as a few eggplants that really needed using up. Scoop this up with warm pita bread (p. 23) and eat it alongside other mezze, or with soft-boiled eggs for a hearty breakfast.

Serves 4, as part of a mezze spread

4 medium eggplants
(2 lb 2 oz/1kg)

3 tbsp olive oil, *plus extra
for greasing*

2 garlic cloves, *thinly sliced*

2 tbsp pine nuts

1½ tsp cumin seeds, *roughly
crushed with a mortar and
pestle*

1½ tsp coriander seeds,
*roughly crushed with a
mortar and pestle*

½ tsp chile flakes

2 tbsp tahini

¼ cup/5g dill, *roughly
chopped, plus 1 tbsp extra
leaves to serve*

TOMATO SAUCE

3 tbsp olive oil

1 onion, *finely chopped*
(1¼ cups/180g)

4 garlic cloves, *minced*

1 tsp tomato paste

**1 (14 oz/400g) can of
whole, peeled tomatoes,**
roughly crushed by hand

½ tsp sugar

salt and black pepper

1. Place a well-greased grill pan on high heat. Prick the eggplants all over with a fork, about 8–10 times, and, once smoking, cook them, turning as necessary until well charred all over and softened through the middle, about 45 minutes. Set aside to cool completely and, once cool enough to handle, peel and discard the stems and skins (don't worry if there's some skin attached) and roughly pull apart the flesh into strands. Set aside.

2. Make the tomato sauce. Put the oil into a sauté pan on medium-high heat. Add the onion and cook for 6 minutes, stirring occasionally, until softened. Add the garlic and tomato paste and cook for a minute more, then add the tomatoes, sugar, 7 tablespoons/100ml of water, ½ teaspoon of salt, and a generous grind of pepper. Bring to a simmer, then lower the heat to medium and cook for 18 minutes, stirring occasionally, until thick and rich.

3. Make the topping. Heat the oil in a small frying pan on medium-high heat, then add the sliced garlic and the pine nuts and cook for 60–90 seconds, or until lightly golden. Add the spices and a tiny pinch of salt and immediately remove from the heat. Set aside.

4. In a small bowl, whisk the tahini with 2½ tablespoons of water and a tiny pinch of salt until smooth and pourable.

5. To the tomato sauce, add the burnt eggplant, 3 tablespoons of water, ¼ teaspoon of salt, and a good grind of pepper and cook on medium-high heat for about 5 minutes, stirring occasionally, until heated through. Remove from the heat and stir in the chopped dill. Drizzle all over with the tahini, then spoon on the fried garlic and pine nut mixture and top with the dill leaves. Serve warm.

Make it your own:
- Save time: Use 2¼ cups/500g jarred tomato sauce instead.
- Replace the burnt eggplant with chopped-up roasted veggies such as zucchini and red bell peppers.

_____

_____

_____

Sweet potato shakshuka with sriracha butter and pickled onions

Prep time: *20 minutes*
Cook time: *1 hour 20 minutes*

A far cry from a classic shakshuka, yes, but we've found that sweet potatoes provide just the right amount of moisture and heft to serve as a base for these eggs. Serve this vibrant dish as a weekend brunch; it sure looks the part.

Serves 4

2 lb 2 oz/1kg sweet
  potatoes, *skin on and
  scrubbed clean*
1 small red onion, *thinly
  sliced into rounds
  (3½ oz/100g)*
2 tbsp lemon juice
3 tbsp olive oil
1⅓ cups/150g coarsely
  grated mature cheddar
3 garlic cloves, *minced*
1 tsp cumin seeds, *roughly
  crushed with a mortar and
  pestle*
8 large eggs
2 tbsp unsalted butter
2¼ tsp sriracha
2 tbsp cilantro leaves, *with
  some stem attached*
salt and black pepper

1. Preheat the oven to 425°F. Poke the sweet potatoes all over with a fork (about 8–10 times) and place them on a medium, parchment-lined baking sheet. Bake for 45–50 minutes, or until cooked through and softened. Set aside to cool and turn the oven temperature down to 400°F.

2. Meanwhile, in a small bowl, mix together the red onion, 1 tablespoon of lemon juice, and a pinch of salt and set aside to pickle.

3. Remove the cooked potato skins and tear them into roughly 1½-inch/4cm pieces. Transfer the potato flesh to a large bowl and set aside. Place the skins back on the baking sheet and toss with 1 tablespoon of oil, ¼ teaspoon of salt, and a good grind of pepper. Bake for 8 minutes, or until nicely colored and starting to crisp up. Set aside to cool and crisp up further.

4. Use a fork to mash the potato flesh until smooth, then add the cheddar, garlic, cumin, another 1 tablespoon of oil, the remaining 1 tablespoon of lemon juice, 1 teaspoon of salt, and a generous grind of pepper, and mix to combine.

5. Put the remaining 1 tablespoon of oil into a large frying pan, for which you have a lid, and swirl around to coat the bottom. Spoon the mashed potato mixture into the pan, using your spoon to distribute it evenly. Place on medium-high heat and let cook for about 7 minutes, for the bottom to start to color. Turn the heat down to medium and use a spoon to make eight wells in the potato mixture, breaking an egg into each. Sprinkle lightly with salt and pepper, cover with the lid, and cook for 4–5 minutes, rotating the pan, or until the whites are set and the yolks are still runny.

6. While the eggs are cooking, put the butter and sriracha into a small saucepan on medium heat and cook until the butter has melted, whisking constantly to emulsify. Remove the mixture from the heat before it starts to bubble—you don't want it to split.

7. When ready, spoon the sriracha butter all over the eggs, then top with a good handful of the crispy potato skins, half the pickled onion, and all the cilantro leaves. Serve right away, with the rest of the potato skins and pickled onion to eat alongside.

Make it your own:

- Save time by cooking the sweet taters in the microwave instead.
- Use any kind of oozy melty cheese and any spice you like for the base.
- Experiment with other hot sauces, such as Tabasco or harissa.

_____

_____

_____

Grilled bread with tomato and fried garlic

Prep time: *10 minutes*
Cook time: *20 minutes*

This is a take on the wonderfully simple (but ever satisfying) Spanish pan con tomate. Beautifully ripe tomatoes and some stale bread are all you need to make this quick and easy starter or side.

Serves 4

6 garlic cloves, *5 thinly sliced and 1 minced*

5 tbsp/75ml olive oil, *plus extra for greasing and brushing*

1 lb 14 oz/850g ripe plum tomatoes

½ tsp chile flakes

1 tbsp red wine vinegar

8 (¾ inch/2cm-thick) slices of stale ciabatta bread (7 oz/200g)

5¼ oz/150g datterini or regular cherry tomatoes

2 tbsp oregano leaves

salt and black pepper

1. Put the sliced garlic and 3 tablespoons of oil into a small frying pan and place it on medium heat. Cook for about 8 minutes, or until the garlic turns lightly golden. Strain the oil through a small sieve set over a bowl, and set both the garlic and oil aside separately.

2. Use a box grater to roughly grate the plum tomatoes (p. 88), discarding the skins. Drain the grated tomato in a sieve set over a bowl for about 5 minutes—you want about 14 oz/400g of grated tomato pulp. Discard (or save for another use) the drained tomato liquid, then put the grated tomato into the bowl and stir in the minced garlic, chile flakes, vinegar, the remaining 2 tablespoons of oil, ¾ teaspoon of salt, and a good grind of pepper.

3. Place a well-greased grill pan on high heat. Brush both sides of the ciabatta slices with a little olive oil to coat and, once the pan is hot, cook for about 90 seconds per side, or until lightly charred and toasty. Do this in about two batches. Next, cook the cherry tomatoes until nicely charred and only just starting to burst a little, about 5 minutes.

4. Place the bread slices so that they're nestled together on a plate and spoon on the grated tomato mixture. Top with the cooked cherry tomatoes and the fried garlic and its oil, then sprinkle with the oregano. Serve right away.

Make it your own:
– Use other breads (such as focaccia or sourdough) and other fresh herbs that need using up.

On grating tomatoes

If you've cooked through an Ottolenghi recipe (or three), you might have noticed that it's not uncommon for our recipes to call upon grating tomatoes. In return, we almost always get asked, but how do you even grate a tomato?

If it's not a technique you're familiar with, then we're here to tell you that grating tomatoes is the surest, fastest way to get all the juicy pulp and seeds—sans skin.

• To grate a tomato all you need is: a **box grater**, and a **wide bowl** to catch the pulp and juice. You might also need a **sieve**, if you want to drain the pulp of any juice.

• Place the grater upright in the bowl and gently push the ripe tomatoes against the coarser side of the grater, and grate until you are left with just skin. Make sure to only go as far as you can (careful of your fingers!). The riper the tomato, the easier it will be to grate. Discard the skin.

• Once you've collected all the grated tomato goodness, you can then use it as a dip as we do for the za'atar parathas (p. 28), as a topping as in the grilled bread with tomato and fried garlic (p. 86), cooked into the base of soups and stews as in the magical chicken and Parmesan soup (p. 143), or simply stirred into dishes for freshness as we do in both the (one jar of) butter beans with preserved lemon, chile, and herb oil (p. 15) and the braised beef short ribs with butter beans and figs (p. 125).

Butternut squash with orange oil and caramelized honey

Prep time: *15 minutes*
Cook time: *40 minutes*
Infusion time: *20 minutes to 1 hour*

This dish is one for the autumn months, the sunset shades of squash, orange, and honey adding warmth to your table. Blitzing olive oil with orange peel is a quick way to infuse the oil used here without having to heat it up or wait very long. Trust us when we say that what makes this dish so memorable is the added details.

Serves 4, as a starter or side

1 butternut squash
(2 lb 7 oz/1.1kg), peeled, halved lengthwise, seeded, and then cut into ½-inch/1cm-thick half-moons (2 lb/900g)

2 tbsp olive oil

¼ tsp freshly grated nutmeg

1½ tbsp honey

1½ tsp apple cider vinegar

1½ oz/40g pecorino, *thinly sliced into ⅟₁₆-inch/¼cm-thick shards*

1½ tbsp oregano leaves, *with some stem attached*

2 tbsp pumpkin seeds (pepitas), *toasted*

salt and black pepper

ORANGE-INFUSED OIL

2 oranges

3 tbsp olive oil

1. Preheat the oven to 500°F or as high as your oven can go.

2. For the infused oil, finely shave the orange peel into strips, giving you 1/2 oz/15g of peel (avoiding any pith). Roughly chop the peel, then transfer to the bowl of a food processor. Add the oil and blitz for 1 minute, or until the peel is finely chopped. Transfer to a bowl and allow to infuse for 20–60 minutes. Strain through a sieve into a separate bowl, discarding the solids.

3. Segment both the peeled oranges; do this over a sieve set over a bowl to catch the juice. Set aside the segments and 1 tablespoon of the collected juice for the dressing.

4. Put the butternut squash, olive oil, nutmeg, ½ teaspoon of salt, and a good grind of pepper into a large bowl, tossing to combine. Divide between two parchment-lined baking sheets, spacing the pieces so that they're not overlapping, and bake for 20–25 minutes, turning the pieces halfway through, until cooked through and nicely browned. Set aside to cool to room temperature.

5. Meanwhile, put the honey into a small frying pan on medium-high heat. Bring to a boil, then cook for 2–3 minutes, stirring occasionally, until the honey turns to a deep brown caramel. Remove from the heat and immediately stir in the orange segments, the 1 tablespoon of reserved juice, and the vinegar. Set aside to cool slightly.

6. Arrange the butternut squash and pecorino on a large platter. Pour the caramelized honey dressing over the top, and top with the oregano, pumpkin seeds, and orange oil.

Make it your own:
– Double or triple the amount of orange oil and keep it in a sealed jar for drizzling over salads, roasted vegetables, or fruit and yogurt.
– Swap out the butternut squash for its other orange friend, the pumpkin.

_____

_____

_____

Lime and poppy seed slaw with curry leaf oil

Prep time: *25 minutes*
Cook time: *40 minutes*

Eat this zingy slaw al fresco, with the spicy vindaloo photographed alongside (p. 110), though it's also just as great on its own. Doubling up the turmeric cashews won't hurt either; they're super-duper special and will keep for up to a week in a sealed container (though we doubt they'll last that long).

Serves 6, as a side

1 white cabbage *(1 lb 14 oz/ 850g), core removed and head finely sliced (7¾ cups/700g)*

1–2 carrots *(6⅓ oz/180g), peeled, halved crosswise, then thinly sliced and julienned*

1 red onion *(4½ oz/120g), halved and very thinly sliced*

¾ cup/15g cilantro leaves, *with some stem attached*

¼ cup/5g mint leaves

salt and black pepper

TURMERIC CASHEWS

2 tbsp light brown sugar

2½ tsp olive oil

¾ tsp ground turmeric

1⅓ cups/200g roasted and salted cashews

2 tsp cumin seeds

CURRY LEAF OIL

1 small Fresno chile, *thinly sliced, seeds and all (2 tbsp/10g)*

3 tbsp olive oil

20 fresh curry leaves *(from 2 sprigs)*

LIME DRESSING

5 tbsp/70ml lime juice *(from about 4 limes)*

2 tsp Dijon mustard

2 garlic cloves, *minced*

1 tbsp poppy seeds

¼ tsp salt

5 tbsp/75ml olive oil

1. Preheat the oven to 350°F. Line a medium baking sheet with parchment paper.

2. Make the turmeric cashews. Put the sugar, oil, turmeric, and 2 tablespoons of water into a small saucepan. Bring to a boil on medium heat, stirring often, then add the cashews and cumin. Cook for another 3–4 minutes, stirring constantly, until the seeds and nuts are coated in a sticky glaze. Transfer to the prepared baking sheet, using a spatula to spread the nuts out. Bake for 14 minutes, stirring once halfway, until golden. Set aside to cool completely.

3. Make the curry leaf oil by putting the chile and oil into a small frying pan. Place it on medium heat and cook for 7 minutes, or until the chile starts to develop a shine, then add the curry leaves and cook for 2–3 minutes more, stirring often, until the leaves turn translucent. Transfer to a bowl and set aside.

4. Make the dressing by putting the lime juice, mustard, garlic, poppy seeds, and ¼ teaspoon of salt into a small bowl and whisking to combine. Slowly drizzle in the olive oil, whisking continuously until incorporated.

5. In a large bowl, combine the cabbage, carrots, onion, ½ teaspoon of salt, and a good grind of pepper. Pour in the dressing, mixing well to combine, and let soften slightly, about 15 minutes. Fold in the cilantro and mint, then transfer to a large serving platter. Drizzle the curry leaf oil all over and sprinkle with a handful of the turmeric cashews, serving the rest in a bowl alongside, to munch on.

Make it your own:

- Play with the nuts. Blanched peanuts or almonds would work just as well here!
- Make the slaw with different cabbages, kohlrabi, and other crunchy veggies.
- Leave out the curry leaves if you can't find them and stir some fresh herbs into the oil instead.

Fennel and zucchini salad
with preserved lemon dressing

Prep time: *35 minutes*
Cook time: *15 minutes*

Every so often, the team will put their heads together and brainstorm recipe ideas. Gitai, listening intently while tapping away at his computer, will let out the occasional murmur of agreement, sigh of disapproval, or chip in with his suggestions. We often joke that fennel salad is Gitai's signature go-to, his love of raw vegetables so very compelling. This salad is dedicated wholeheartedly to Gitai, who has contributed plenty of inspired ideas to the recipes developed at the OTK.

Serve this on a hot summer's day, alongside a summery spread and a chilled glass of wine. You can make the dressing well in advance, but don't mix everything together until just before serving; it releases water as it sits.

Serves 4, as a side

1 cup/20g mint leaves, *chopped*

1 cup/20g dill, *chopped*

scant 1 oz/25g chives, *cut into ¾-inch/2cm lengths*

5 tbsp/75ml olive oil

2 large fennel bulbs *(1 lb 10 oz/750g), trimmed, halved lengthwise, and finely shaved on a mandolin or by hand*

2 zucchini *(15 oz/420g), trimmed and finely shaved on a mandolin or by hand*

1 tbsp lemon juice

1½ tsp fennel seeds, *toasted and roughly crushed with a mortar and pestle*

1½ tsp pink peppercorns, *roughly crushed with a mortar and pestle*

salt and black pepper

DRESSING

1½ oz/40g preserved lemon *(1–2 lemons), seeds discarded and flesh chopped (3 tbsp)*

½ small shallot, *chopped*

1 garlic clove, *minced*

1½ tbsp lemon juice

2½ tbsp olive oil

1. Make the dressing by putting the preserved lemon, shallot, garlic, and lemon juice into the small bowl of a food processor and blitzing until finely chopped. With the machine running, gradually add the oil and blitz for 1–2 minutes more, until completely smooth. Transfer to a small bowl.

2. Put all the herbs, 4 tablespoons of oil, and a pinch each of salt and pepper into the food processor and pulse to finely chop.

3. Add the fennel, zucchini, lemon juice, ⅔ teaspoon of salt, and a good grind of pepper to a large bowl and mix well to combine. Set aside for 5 minutes to soften, then add the herb mixture and toss together well.

4. Transfer half the salad to a large plate, and spoon half the dressing and half the fennel seeds and pink peppercorns over the top. Repeat once more, drizzle with the last 1 tablespoon of oil, and serve right away.

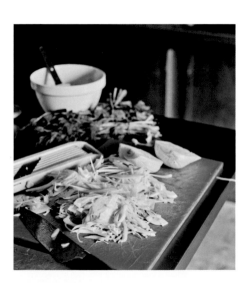

Grilled confit parsnips
with herbs and vinegar

Prep time: *20 minutes*
Cook time: *1 hour 20 minutes*

Good old parsnips, the most underrated of root vegetables, making their appearance on the odd occasion but not nearly enough. Here they are given some extra love and attention: first by letting them cook slowly and gently in oil, then by grilling them for that smoky hit. Save the flavorful oil that you're left with—use it to dress salads or to drizzle over dips or mezze.

Serves 4–6, as a side

2 small Fresno chiles, *thinly sliced at a slight angle (¼ cup/20g), seeded if you don't like heat*

3 tbsp apple cider vinegar

1 lb 10 oz/750g medium parsnips, *peeled and halved lengthwise*

11 garlic cloves, *peeled, 10 left whole and 1 minced*

1¾ cups/450ml olive oil

¾ cup/15g cilantro, *roughly chopped*

½ cup/10g parsley, *roughly chopped*

1 tsp ground allspice

flaked sea salt and black pepper

1. Preheat the oven to 350°F. Put the chiles, vinegar, and a small pinch of flaked salt into a medium bowl. Allow to pickle lightly.

2. Put the parsnips, 10 garlic cloves, oil, and 1 tablespoon of flaked salt into a high-sided baking dish about 12 x 8 inches/ 30 x 20cm in size. Cover tightly with foil, then transfer to the oven to bake for 1 hour, or until a knife slides easily into the thicker part of the parsnips. Remove the parsnips and garlic, reserving the oil.

3. Place a well-greased grill pan on high heat and ventilate your kitchen well. Once hot, cook the parsnips in 2–3 batches, until deeply charred on both sides, about 2–3 minutes per batch. Transfer to a large bowl (or dish) while you continue with the rest. Cook the garlic cloves for 1 minute until charred, then transfer to the bowl of parsnips.

4. Put the herbs, minced garlic, ¼ cup/60ml of the reserved parsnip oil, ¼ teaspoon of flaked salt, and a good grind of pepper into the bowl of a food processor and blitz until finely chopped.

5. Add the herb mixture, pickled chiles, and allspice to the parsnip bowl, tossing gently to combine, then transfer to a large serving platter. Drizzle with 2 more tablespoons of the parsnip oil and serve warm or at room temperature.

Make it your own:
- Skip the grilling and roast the confit parsnips in a hot oven until nicely colored.
- Try this technique with other root vegetables, such as potatoes or turnips, adjusting the cooking times as necessary.

_____

_____

_____

Brussels sprout and Parmesan salad with lemon dressing

Prep time: *25 minutes*
Cook time: *35 minutes*

We would encourage you to eat your Brussels with plenty of texture (well roasted or raw) and coated in punchy flavors, such as salty Parmesan, umami anchovies, and spicy mustard. Serve this salad as a side to a Sunday roast or do what we did and eat it alongside the cheesy polenta and tomato sauce (p. 24).

Serves 4, as a side

- **1 lb 9 oz/700g small Brussels sprouts,** *trimmed, 1 lb 2 oz/500g left whole and 7 oz/200g thinly shaved on a mandolin or by hand*
- **8 tbsp/120ml olive oil,** *plus extra for drizzling*
- **¼ cup/60ml lemon juice**
- **3 garlic cloves,** *minced*
- **1½ tbsp whole grain mustard**
- **2 anchovies in oil,** *drained and roughly chopped*
- **2¼ oz/60g Parmesan,** *¾ oz/20g coarsely grated (3 tbsp) and the rest cut into thin shards*
- **4¼ oz/120g kale leaves,** *stems discarded and leaves thinly sliced (1½ cups/100g)*
- **1 small red onion,** *halved and thinly sliced (3 oz/80g)*
- **1 cup/20g basil leaves**
- **½ cup/70g blanched hazelnuts,** *well toasted and roughly chopped*
- **salt and black pepper**

1. Preheat the oven to 450°F.

2. Put the whole Brussels sprouts, 2 tablespoons of oil, ½ teaspoon of salt, and a good grind of pepper on a parchment-lined baking sheet and mix to combine. Roast for 18 minutes, stirring halfway, until well browned and cooked through. Let cool.

3. Make the dressing by putting the lemon juice, garlic, mustard, anchovies, grated Parmesan, the remaining 6 tablespoons/90ml of oil, ¼ teaspoon of salt, and a good grind of pepper into the bowl of a food processor and blitzing until smooth.

4. Put the kale, the thinly shaved raw Brussels sprouts, the dressing, ¼ teaspoon of salt, and a good grind of pepper into a large mixing bowl and toss together well, massaging the leaves a little. Allow to soften and wilt slightly, about 10 minutes.

5. To the bowl add the onion, basil, chopped hazelnuts, Parmesan shards, and roasted Brussels sprouts and mix to combine. Pile onto a large serving dish.

Make it your own:
- Lose the fish: swap out the anchovies for capers.
- Use other cabbage, such as sweetheart/hispi cabbage, instead of Brussels sprouts.

_____

_____

Who
does
the

Dishes
Dishes
Dishes
Dishes
Dishes
Dishes
Dishes
Dishes
Dishes
Dishes
Dishes
Dishes

Who does the dishes

There's a point during the day—around late afternoon—once our trials have been tested and tasted, our recipes modified and tweaked, when the dish area starts to look a little too full, the plates piled a little too high and the sink a little too ready to be soaped down. It's at this point that one-pan dishes are a welcome addition to our repertoire, but this chapter isn't really about the washing-up (although fewer dishes is always an added bonus).

Who does the dishes is all about cooking things in one pan, one baking sheet, one dish—a single vessel for all the ingredients to hang out in, get to know one another and then, once they're comfortable, to soften and let their guard down. Eventually, and as they cook down, the individual ingredients begin to give a little—releasing their unique properties unto each other and morphing into their collective purpose. This character-building softens their cores and hardens their exteriors, forming golden shades of delicious personality. At times they'll need a little bit of help to get them going—a stir, a nudge, a 180° turn—but you can mostly leave them to their own devices.

The confit tandoori chickpeas (p. 105) is perhaps our best example of a one-pan dish with minimal effort, maximum oomph. Our favorite little bean comes together with its animated friends—ginger, garlic, spices!—and, given the right environment, transforms into an intensely flavored dish to be mopped up with bread or rice or simply dug into with a spoon (and an appetite). The 5-a-day toad-in-the-hole (p. 106) needs a little more maintenance, a delicate balance of timing and temperature, but is worth it for the end result of puffed-up, crispy batter and soft, beet-stained root veggies.

We've included this chapter in the book for several reasons, the most important of all being that, of all the recipes out there, one-pan bakes get the majority vote in many a popularity contest. The second being that a raid-your-shelves book can only be improved with a "then throw it into a pot" instruction. Love your shelves, but also love that there's a lot less washing-up too!

Confit tandoori chickpeas

Prep time: *25 minutes*
Cook time: *1 hour 20 minutes*

These tandoori-spiced chickpeas have had their fair share of Insta fame for a multitude of reasons. The first being that the simplicity of the dish makes it really quite attractive: throw everything into a pan and pop it into the oven, leaving it to its own devices (and you to yours). The second being that slow-cooking the chickpeas in oil without added liquid makes them super soft, allowing all the aromatics to break down into the oil. Lastly, this dish can easily be made ahead and served later; it only improves with time. Swap out Greek yogurt with a non-dairy alternative for a completely vegan meal, and serve with rice.

Serves 4

2 (15 oz/425g) cans of chickpeas, *drained (17 oz/480g total)*

11 garlic cloves, *peeled, 10 left whole and 1 minced*

1 oz/30g fresh ginger, *peeled and julienned*

14 oz/400g datterini or regular cherry tomatoes

3 small Fresno chiles, *mild or spicy, a slit cut down their length*

1 tbsp tomato paste

2 tsp cumin seeds, *roughly crushed with a mortar and pestle*

2 tsp coriander seeds, *roughly crushed with a mortar and pestle*

½ tsp ground turmeric

½ tsp chile flakes

2 tsp red Kashmiri chile powder

1 tsp sugar

¾ cup plus 2 tbsp/200ml olive oil

⅔ cup/180g Greek yogurt

¾ cup/15g mint leaves

1½ cups/30g cilantro, *roughly chopped*

2–3 limes: *juiced to get 1 tbsp and the rest cut into wedges to serve*

salt

1. Preheat the oven to 350°F.

2. Put the chickpeas, whole garlic cloves, ginger, tomatoes, chiles, tomato paste, spices, sugar, oil, and 1 teaspoon of salt into a large, oven-safe sauté pan, for which you have a lid, and mix everything together to combine. Cover with the lid, transfer to the oven and cook for 75 minutes, stirring halfway through, until the aromatics have softened and the tomatoes have nicely broken down.

3. Meanwhile, put the yogurt, mint, cilantro, lime juice, minced garlic, and ¼ teaspoon of salt into a food processor and blitz until smooth and the herbs are finely chopped.

4. Serve the chickpeas directly from the pan, with the yogurt and lime wedges alongside.

Make it your own:

– Jarred or canned butter beans (lima beans) would be great here!
– No Kashmiri chile powder? Use an equal amount of paprika instead.

_____

_____

_____

_____

5-a-day toad-in-the-hole

Prep time: *30 minutes*
Cook time: *1 hour 40 minutes*
Resting time: *30 minutes*

BATTER

4 large eggs

1½ cups/360ml whole milk

2 tbsp English mustard

1¾ cups plus 1 tbsp/230g
all-purpose flour, *sifted*

1 tsp salt

¼ cup vegetable oil

FILLING

½ large celeriac *(1 lb 1 oz/*
480g), peeled and cut into
6 wedges (1 lb/450g)

12¼ oz/350g beets *(about 2),*
peeled and each cut into
8 wedges (10½ oz/300g)

½ large rutabaga *(12¼ oz/*
350g), peeled and cut into
12 wedges (11¼ oz/320g)

5 tbsp/75ml olive oil

2 tbsp tomato paste

2 tbsp maple syrup

7 oz/200g datterini or
cherry tomatoes

2 rosemary sprigs

salt and black pepper

MUSHROOM GRAVY
(OPTIONAL)

1 oz/30g dried porcini
mushrooms

3⅓ cups/800ml boiling
water

2 tbsp olive oil

1 large onion, *finely chopped*

3 garlic cloves, *minced*

1 tbsp tomato paste

1 tbsp finely chopped
rosemary leaves

2½ tbsp all-purpose flour

1 tbsp balsamic vinegar

¼ oz/5g chives, *sliced into*
½-inch/1cm lengths

This vegetarian take on the classic dish features five different vegetables, which, in our terms, counts toward the prerequisite five servings of fruits and vegetables per day. The trick here is to get the oil very hot before pouring in the batter, working very quickly to get it back into the oven as soon as possible—allowing for the batter to rise and puff up as it should. Making your own gravy means using a few more dishes, but we think it is truly worth it.

Serves 4–6

1. Preheat the oven to 425°F.

2. Put the dried mushrooms and boiling water into a heatproof bowl. Cover with a plate and let them steep for at least 20 minutes.

3. Make the batter by putting the eggs, milk, and mustard into a large bowl and whisking vigorously until foamy, about 1 minute. Put the flour and salt into a separate large bowl, then pour in the egg mixture. Whisk until smooth and no lumps remain. Set aside for 30 minutes.

4. Put all the root vegetables, the olive oil, tomato paste, ¾ teaspoon of salt, and a good grind of pepper into a large roasting pan, roughly 9 x 13 inches/23 x 33 cm. Roast for 20 minutes, then stir in the maple syrup. Return to the oven for 15 minutes more, until softened and nicely colored. Transfer the vegetables and flavorful oil to a bowl and give the roasting pan a good rinse and dry.

5. Add the vegetable oil to the wiped-out roasting pan and place in the oven for 6 minutes, to heat up. Working quickly and very carefully, remove the hot pan from the oven and pour in the batter. Top evenly with the

roasted vegetables and their oil, the cherry tomatoes, and the rosemary sprigs. Return to the oven for 20 minutes, then lower the heat to 400°F and cook for 25 minutes more.

6. Meanwhile, make the gravy. Heat the oil in a medium saucepan on medium-high heat, then add the onion and cook for 7 minutes, stirring occasionally, until softened and browned. Add the garlic, tomato paste, and rosemary and cook for 1 minute more. Add the flour, stirring to coat, then slowly pour in the steeped porcini mushrooms and their liquid, stirring constantly to avoid lumps. Add 1 teaspoon of salt and a generous grind of pepper and bring to a simmer. Lower the heat to medium and cook for 12 minutes, then add the vinegar and cook for 5 minutes more, or until thickened to a gravy. Keep warm until ready to serve.

7. Stir two-thirds of the chives into the gravy and sprinkle the rest over the toad-in-the-hole. Serve warm, with the gravy to pour alongside.

> **Make it your own:**
>
> - Feel free to use a store-bought gravy to save time (and washing-up).
> - Play around by using your favorite root vegetables.
>
> _____
>
> _____
>
> _____

Spicy pulled pork vindaloo

Prep time: *20 minutes*
Cook time: *6 hours*
15 minutes

When feeding a crowd, we are huge fans of large cuts of meat or large whole vegetables, slow-cooked with minimal work and maximum flavor. The most work involved here is making the Indian vindaloo paste, a small ask for a dish that packs a serious kick. Serve this pork with the lime and poppy seed slaw with curry leaf oil (p. 92), or with a good-quality store-bought slaw.

Serves 8

3 cinnamon sticks,
  roughly broken
15 cardamom pods
1½ tsp black peppercorns
10 dried Kashmiri chiles,
  stems removed
1½ tbsp cumin seeds
2 tsp black mustard seeds
¼ tsp ground cloves
10 garlic cloves, *peeled*
1¾ oz/50g fresh ginger,
  peeled and roughly chopped
1 tbsp sugar
2 tbsp tomato paste
6 tbsp/90ml apple cider
  vinegar
½ cup plus 2 tbsp/150ml
  full-fat coconut milk
4¾ lb/2.2kg pork shoulder,
  rolled and boneless
3 tbsp vegetable oil
3 onions, *roughly chopped*
  (3 cups/450g)
1 cup/20g cilantro,
  roughly chopped
2 tbsp lime juice
salt and black pepper

TO SERVE
1¾ cups/500g Greek yogurt
6 tbsp/120g mango
  chutney, *store-bought*
8 white soft bread rolls,
  store-bought

1. Put the first 13 ingredients into a medium bowl and mix to combine. Let soak for 30 minutes, then transfer to a food processor or blender and blitz until smooth, 3–4 minutes.

2. Preheat the oven to 350°F.

3. Pat dry the pork, then sprinkle all over with 1 teaspoon of salt. Put 2 tablespoons of oil into a large Dutch oven on medium-high heat. Add the pork and sear to lightly brown on all sides, about 8 minutes. Remove the pork and set aside. Add the remaining 1 tablespoon of oil and the onions, stirring to lightly color, about 3 minutes, then add the blitzed spice mixture, 1¾ cups/450ml of water, and 1 teaspoon of salt. Return the pork to the pan, bring to a boil,

then cover with the lid and transfer to the oven to bake for 4 hours, basting every 1 hour or so. Remove the lid and return to the oven for 80 minutes more, basting once or twice throughout, until browned and the sauce is thick and rich.

4. Use two forks to shred the pork directly in the pan with all its juices. You can choose to shred the skin as well, or discard it. Stir in the cilantro and lime juice.

5. Place the yogurt in a small bowl and swirl in the chutney. Serve this and the bread rolls alongside the pork, building your own plate or sandwich as you please.

Get ahead:
 – Make the whole thing the day before you want to serve it, reheating the pulled pork on the stovetop.

Make it your own:

– Not into heat? Use half the amount of chile asked for.
– Use any dried mild red chile in place of dried Kashmiri chiles.
– Swap out the pork for rolled boneless lamb shoulder, keeping an eye on cooking times.

Baked orzo puttanesca

Prep time: *15 minutes*
Cook time: *50 minutes*

This is a one-pot meal in its own right, but also a bit of a kitchen raid, using up cans, jars, and packages from your cupboards and a few bits from the fridge as well.

Serves 4

4 tbsp/60ml olive oil

1 onion, *finely chopped (1 cup/150g)*

6 garlic cloves, *minced*

½ tsp chile flakes

3 anchovies in oil, *drained and roughly chopped*

2 tbsp capers

1 oz/30g preserved lemon, *inner parts discarded and skin thinly sliced into strips (1 tbsp)*

½ cup/70g pitted Kalamata olives, *roughly torn in half*

2 (5-oz/140g) cans of good-quality tuna in olive oil, *drained and roughly flaked*

1 tbsp tomato paste

1 (14 oz/400g) can of diced tomatoes

1⅓ cups/250g dried orzo

1–2 plum tomatoes *(6⅓ oz/180g), cored and cut into ¼-inch/½cm-thick rounds*

⅓ cup/40g finely grated Parmesan

¼ cup/5g basil leaves, *roughly torn*

salt and black pepper

1. Preheat the oven to 425°F.

2. Put 3 tablespoons of oil into a large, oven-safe sauté pan, for which you have a lid, on medium-high heat. Add the onion and cook for 8 minutes, stirring occasionally, until softened and browned. Add the garlic, chile, and anchovies and cook for 1 minute more, until fragrant. Stir in the capers, half the preserved lemon, ⅓ cup/45g of olives, the tuna, tomato paste, canned tomatoes, orzo, 1¾ cups/450ml of water, 1 teaspoon of salt, and a generous grind of pepper. Bring to a simmer, then cover with the lid and bake for 20 minutes, until the orzo is cooked through.

3. Turn the oven temperature up to 475°F. Remove the lid, top with the sliced tomatoes, sprinkle with the cheese, and bake for 10–12 minutes more, until lightly browned. Let sit for 10 minutes.

4. Top with the remaining olives and preserved lemon, the basil leaves, and the remaining 1 tablespoon of oil.

Make it your own:

– Lose the fish: swap out the canned tuna for jarred artichoke hearts and the anchovies for more capers.

_____

_____

_____

_____

_____

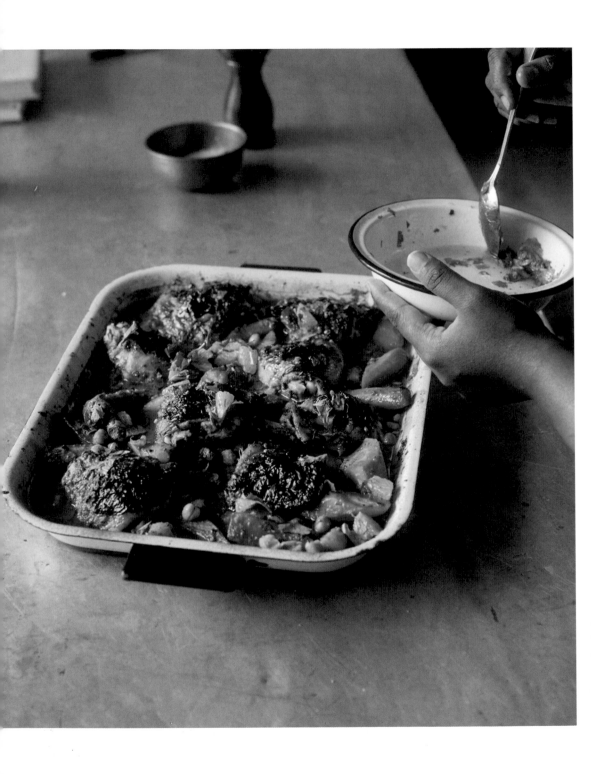

Berbere spiced chicken, carrots, and chickpeas

Prep time: *25 minutes*
Cook time: *1 hour 25 minutes*

Berbere is an Ethiopian spice blend with quite a bit of a kick, so use a little less if you're not into heat. We use store-bought berbere spice, but you can also toast and grind your own homemade blend, especially if you have a well-stocked spice rack. We love this for being a complete meal in one pan, but wouldn't say no to a big ol' bowl of greens to eat alongside.

Serves 4–6

1 large onion, *roughly chopped (1½ cups/220g)*

6 garlic cloves, *peeled*

2¼ cups/45g cilantro, *stalks (1¼ cups/25g) and leaves (1 cup/20g) separated and roughly chopped*

2½ tbsp berbere spice

2 tbsp tomato paste

2½ tbsp honey, *plus a little extra for drizzling*

3 tbsp apple cider vinegar

6 tbsp/90ml olive oil

1¾ lb/800g carrots, *peeled and cut into 1½–2-inch/4–5cm lengths (1½ lb/680g)*

2 (15 oz/425g) cans of chickpeas, *drained (17 oz/480g total)*

8 medium chicken thighs, *skin on and bone in*

2–3 oranges: *1 left whole and the rest juiced to get 7 tbsp/100ml*

salt and black pepper

1. Preheat the oven to 425°F.

2. Put the onion, garlic, cilantro stalks, berbere spice, tomato paste, honey, 1 tablespoon of vinegar, 4 tablespoons of oil, 1¾ teaspoons of salt, and a good grind of black pepper into a food processor and blitz to a smooth paste.

3. Put the blitzed onion mixture, carrots, chickpeas, chicken, orange juice, and ½ cup plus 2 tablespoons/150ml of water into a large roasting pan, roughly 13 x 10 inches/34 x 26cm in size, and toss everything together to combine. Arrange the thighs so that they're skin side up and slightly nestled on top, then cover the dish tightly with foil and bake for 30 minutes. Remove the foil and return to the oven for 40 minutes more, rotating the pan halfway through, or until everything is cooked through and

nicely colored. Set aside to settle slightly, about 10 minutes.

4. Meanwhile, peel and segment the whole orange and then roughly chop the flesh. Put this into a medium bowl along with the chopped cilantro leaves, the remaining 2 tablespoons of vinegar, the remaining 2 tablespoons of oil, and a pinch each of salt and pepper, and mix to combine.

5. When ready to serve, spoon the cilantro sauce all over the top and serve directly from the roasting pan.

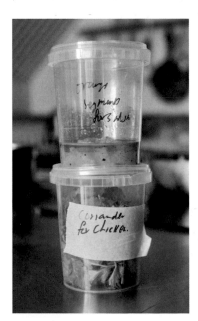

Make it your own:
- Swap out the berbere spice for other spice blends such as hawaij (p. 16).
- Use other chicken segments if you prefer.

Za'atar salmon and tahini

Prep time: *5 minutes*
Cook time: *20 minutes*

If you haven't yet paired fish with tahini, then you're in for a real treat. This version combines tahini with herbaceous za'atar and sour sumac, our ever familiar but much treasured test kitchen staples. We strongly recommend using creamy, nutty tahini that's sourced from countries within the Levant. Eat this shortly after cooking, as cooked tahini doesn't sit or reheat very well.

Serves 4

4 salmon fillets *(1 lb 5 oz/ 600g), skin on and pin bones removed*

2 tbsp za'atar

2 tsp sumac, *plus ½ tsp extra for sprinkling*

4 tbsp/60ml olive oil

9 oz/250g baby spinach

⅓ cup/90g tahini

3 garlic cloves, *minced*

3½ tbsp lemon juice

1½ tbsp roughly chopped cilantro leaves

salt and black pepper

1. Preheat the oven to 450°F.

2. Pat dry the salmon and sprinkle with salt and pepper. In a small bowl, combine the za'atar and sumac, then sprinkle this all over the top of the salmon to create a crust.

3. Place a large, oven-safe sauté pan on medium-high heat and add 1 tablespoon of oil. Once hot, add the spinach and a pinch each of salt and pepper and cook for 2–3 minutes, until just wilted.

4. Top with the salmon, skin side down, and drizzle the top of the fish with 2 tablespoons of oil. Bake for 5 minutes.

5. Meanwhile, in a small bowl whisk together the tahini, garlic, 2½ tablespoons of lemon juice, a good pinch of salt, and 7 tablespoons/100ml of water until smooth and quite runny.

6. When ready, remove the pan from the oven and pour the tahini all around the salmon (but not on the fish at all). Bake for another 5 minutes, or until the fish is cooked through and the tahini is bubbling. Spoon the remaining 1 tablespoon each of lemon juice and oil over everything and top with the cilantro and extra sumac.

Make it your own:

– Swap out the salmon for other sustainably caught fish, adjusting cooking times as needed.
– Use other leafy greens in place of spinach, such as kale or chard.

_____

_____

_____

_____

Chickpeas cacio e pepe

Prep time: *20 minutes*
Cook time: *2 hours
10 minutes*
Soaking time: *overnight*

These chickpeas are inspired by cacio e pepe, a rich Italian dish of pasta coated in lavish amounts of butter, black pepper, and cheese. This uses a similar technique applied to our favorite little bean, using the flavorful Parmesan chickpea water to create the emulsified sauce. Chickpeas differ in size depending on where you are in the world, so if you feel that this should be a little looser, just add a splash of water. Be sure to start the night before by soaking the chickpeas.

Serves 4

1½ cups/300g dried chickpeas, *soaked overnight in plenty of water and 1 tsp baking soda*

3 tbsp olive oil

8 garlic cloves, *minced*

¾ cup/80g finely grated Parmesan, *plus 1–2 optional Parmesan rinds*

¼ tsp baking soda

2 small Fresno chiles, *thinly sliced into rounds, seeds and all*

2 tbsp apple cider vinegar

9 oz/250g baby spinach

¾ cup/15g parsley, *roughly chopped*

7 tbsp/100g unsalted butter, *fridge cold and cut into ¾–inch/2cm cubes*

salt and black pepper

1. Preheat the oven to 350°F.

2. Drain the chickpeas well and set them aside. Put 2 tablespoons of oil into a large Dutch oven and place on medium-high heat. Once hot, add the garlic and cook for 90 seconds, until starting to color. Add the Parmesan rinds, if using, the drained chickpeas, baking soda, 5 cups/1.2 liters of water, and a very generous amount of coarsely cracked black pepper (give it about 40 grinds). Bring to a boil, skimming the scum from the surface as needed, then cover with the lid and bake in the oven for 75 minutes. Add ¾ teaspoon of salt and continue cooking, covered, for another 30 minutes, or until the chickpeas are very soft and the liquid has reduced by about half.

3. Meanwhile, mix together the chiles, vinegar, and a small pinch of salt in a small bowl. Set aside to pickle.

4. Toward the last 10 minutes of cooking the chickpeas, put the last 1 tablespoon of oil into a large frying pan on medium-high heat and, once hot, cook the spinach, adding it to the pan in

batches with ¼ teaspoon of salt until just wilted, about 4 minutes. Add the parsley and remove from the heat.

5. When the chickpeas are ready, remove the lid and, while still hot from the oven but off the heat, add a quarter of the butter cubes and about 2 tablespoons of grated Parmesan, mixing until the butter has melted into the sauce. Continue in this way, adding a quarter more of the butter and 2 tablespoons more of Parmesan until you've used up all 7 tablespoons/100g of butter and ½ cup/60g of cheese. Finally, add another very generous grind of coarsely ground black pepper. The sauce will have thickened significantly, coating the chickpeas nicely. Add a splash more water if you like it looser. Remove the Parmesan rinds, if using.

6. Top with the spinach mixture, the pickled chiles and their liquid, and a final sprinkling of Parmesan, serving any extra grated Parmesan alongside.

Make it your own:

- Swap out the pickled chiles for a squeeze of lemon instead.
- Serve with any greens, such as chard or broccolini.
- Use cannellini or butter beans (lima beans), adjusting liquid levels.

_____

_____

_____

One-pan crispy spaghetti and chicken

Prep time: *30 minutes*
Cook time: *1 hour*

Yotam tested this dish out on his two little ones, the most brutally honest of critics, who were so keen that they asked for it two nights in a row—a true testament to midweek dinner success. To top this off, it is easy to prepare and fun to eat and doesn't call upon any hard-to-source ingredients. Cooking the spaghetti in this way lends plenty of texture, allowing for crispier bits around the edges and softer bits throughout.

Serves 4

2 tbsp olive oil

6 chicken thighs, *skin on and bone in (1 lb 9 oz/700g)*

1 large onion, *cut into ½-inch/1cm dice (1½ cups/220g)*

4 garlic cloves, *minced*

2 tbsp thyme leaves

3 tbsp tomato paste

9 oz/250g dried spaghetti, *broken into thirds*

¼ cup/20g finely grated Parmesan

¼ cup/20g fresh breadcrumbs, *finely blitzed*

½ cup/10g parsley, *finely chopped*

1½ tsp finely grated lemon zest

salt and black pepper

1. Preheat the oven to 425°F.

2. Put 1 tablespoon of oil into a large, oven-safe sauté pan, for which you have a lid, and place on high heat. Season the chicken with ¾ teaspoon of salt and plenty of pepper and add to the hot oil, skin side down. Let cook for 7 minutes, without turning over, to brown well.

3. Turn the heat down to medium-high, then add the onion and stir, turning the chicken over. Cook for 5 minutes, until the onion has softened and is lightly browned. Add the garlic, 1 tablespoon of thyme, and all the tomato paste and cook, stirring, for 1 minute more. Arrange the chicken skin side up, add ½ cup plus 2 tablespoons/150ml of water and cook for 10 minutes, stirring occasionally, until most of the liquid has reduced. Add another 1¾ cups/450ml of water, ½ teaspoon salt, and a good grind of pepper, then add the spaghetti, stirring to submerge and evenly distribute it. Use tongs to lift the chicken pieces so that they sit on top of the spaghetti, skin side up. Bring to a simmer, cover with the lid, and bake in the oven for 30 minutes, at which stage all the liquid should have been absorbed.

4. Meanwhile, in a small bowl mix together the Parmesan, breadcrumbs, parsley, lemon zest, and the remaining 1 tablespoon of thyme.

5. After 30 minutes in the oven, remove the pasta pan and reset the oven broiler to high. Sprinkle the breadcrumb mix over the pasta and chicken, drizzle with the remaining oil, and broil for 3–4 minutes, until nicely browned and crisp. Allow to settle for 5 minutes before serving warm, directly from the pan.

Make it your own:
  – Use up any soft herbs or hard cheeses you have on hand.
  – Add some spice and chile heat if making an adult version.

_____

_____

_____

124

Braised beef short ribs
with butter beans and figs

Prep time: *25 minutes*
Cook time: *4 hours*
10 minutes

This is a braise for the winter months, when fall-off-the-bone ribs and warming spices are what you're craving. Don't be intimidated by the long cooking time here—it's mostly a waiting game once the pot goes into the oven, so it can easily be put together in the afternoon, ready for a decadent dinner.

Serves 4

2 onions, *roughly chopped (2 cups/300g)*

6 garlic cloves, *peeled*

1½-inch/4cm piece of fresh ginger, *peeled and roughly chopped (2 tbsp/25g)*

2 small serrano chiles, *roughly chopped, seeds and all (⅓ cup/30g)*

6 beef short ribs *(3⅓ lb/1.5kg)*

¼ cup/60ml olive oil

4 whole star anise

10 cardamom pods, *roughly bashed open with a mortar and pestle*

1½ tbsp tomato paste

2 tsp ground allspice

2 tsp ground cumin

5–6 large plum tomatoes *(1 lb 5 oz/600g), two-thirds roughly chopped and the rest roughly grated (p. 88) and skins discarded*

3½ oz/100g soft dried figs, *roughly chopped into ½-inch/1½cm pieces*

25 oz/700g canned or jarred butter beans (lima beans), *drained (19 oz/550g)*

1 oz/30g chives, *very finely chopped*

1½ tbsp lemon juice

10½ oz/300g large-leaf spinach, *stems discarded and leaves roughly torn (4⅓ cups/130g)*

salt and black pepper

1. Preheat the oven to 350°F.

2. Put the onions, garlic, ginger, and chiles into a food processor, and pulse until very finely chopped.

3. Pat dry the short ribs and lightly sprinkle them all over with salt and pepper. Put 2 tablespoons of oil into a large Dutch oven on medium-high heat. Fry the short ribs in two batches until deeply golden on all sides, about 4 minutes per batch. Remove the ribs and set aside.

4. Add the onion mixture to the saucepan along with the star anise and cardamom, and cook for 5 minutes to soften, stirring occasionally. Add the tomato paste, ground spices, chopped tomatoes, 1½ teaspoons of salt, and a good grind of pepper and cook for 4 minutes more, until the tomatoes start to break down. Add the short ribs and 4⅔ cups/1.1 liters of water, bring to a boil, then cover with the lid and transfer to the oven. Cook for 3 hours, stirring a few times throughout.

5. Add the figs and cook for 30 minutes more, or until the figs have softened and the meat is very tender.

6. Toward the last 20 minutes of cooking, heat the butter beans in a saucepan with enough water to cover and a pinch of salt. Gently simmer for about 15 minutes, then drain off the liquid. Stir in the chives, the remaining 2 tablespoons of oil, the lemon juice, and a good grind of pepper.

7. When ready, remove the short ribs from the pan, gently tugging at the bones to pull them away from the meat; discard the bones and set the meat aside.

8. Heat the sauce and stir in the spinach leaves to wilt, about 3 minutes. Add the grated tomato and remove from the heat.

9. Spoon the sauce into a large shallow platter and top with the beans and beef.

Sweet spiced mushroom and rice pilaf

Prep time: *25 minutes*
Cook time: *1 hour*
55 minutes

This robust vegan main scores major points for its liberal use of warming spices and both fresh and dried mushrooms. It's really quite a festive dish, suitable for the cooler months, and would need nothing more than some lightly cooked greens to eat alongside, or the butternut squash with orange oil (p. 91), for a very happy spread.

Serves 4 as a main, or 6 as a side

1–2 dried ancho chiles
  (½ oz/15g), stems removed
1 oz/30g dried porcini mushrooms
2 cups/480ml vegetable stock, *or chicken stock, if not vegan*
1 lb 2 oz/500g oyster mushrooms,
  left whole
1 lb 2 oz/500g large portobello mushrooms, *stems discarded, each mushroom roughly broken by hand into 6 chunks*
1 large onion, *halved and cut into ¼-inch/½cm-thick slices*
10 garlic cloves, *peeled*
3 cinnamon sticks
4 whole star anise
5¼ oz/150g soft dried apricots *(the plump orange kind), quartered*
½ cup plus 2 tbsp/150ml olive oil
1¾ cups/350g basmati rice, *washed until the water runs clear and drained well*
4 green onions, *thinly sliced at an angle (½ cup/40g)*
¼ cup/5g parsley leaves, *with some stem attached*
salt and black pepper

1. Preheat the oven to 450°F.

2. Put the ancho chiles into a heatproof bowl and pour in enough boiling water to cover. Rehydrate for 20 minutes, then drain off the soaking liquid (save it for another use) and roughly chop the chiles, seeds and all.

3. Meanwhile, put the dried mushrooms, stock, 1½ cups/360ml of water, 1¼ teaspoons of salt, and a good grind of pepper into a medium saucepan on medium-high heat. Bring to a simmer, then set aside.

4. Put the oyster and portobello mushrooms, onion, garlic, chopped chiles, whole spices, apricots, ½ cup/120ml of oil, 1 teaspoon of salt, and a good grind of pepper into a roasting pan about 13 x 10 inches/34 x 26cm in size. Give everything a good stir, then bake for 40 minutes, stirring halfway through, until well browned.

5. Remove from the oven and transfer about half the mixture to a medium bowl. Stir the rice into the remaining mixture in the roasting pan, and set aside.

6. Bring the porcini mixture back up to a simmer. Pour this over the rice mixture and, without stirring, cover the pan tightly with foil. Bake for 25 minutes, until the rice is cooked through. Let rest, covered, for 10 minutes. Remove the foil and gently mix everything together.

7. Add the green onions, parsley, and remaining 2 tablespoons of oil to the reserved mushroom mixture, stirring to combine. Spoon this over the rice and serve.

Make it your own:
– Play around with other types of foraged finds, breaking them up into large chunks to keep intact their naturally "meaty" integrity.
– Use other dried chiles in place of the ancho, such as cascabel or chipotle.

Charred tomatoes, onions, and peppers with feta and harissa pine nuts

Prep time: *30 minutes*
Cook time: *1 hour 15 minutes*

This lands somewhere between a sauce and a dip, great on its own with warm flatbreads but would work just as well spooned on top of pasta, rice, or baked potatoes.

Serves 4

5 tbsp/75ml olive oil

4 small red onions, *each cut into 8 wedges (1 lb 1 oz/480g)*

2 green jalapeños, *stems discarded and flesh chopped into ½-inch/1cm-thick rounds*

2 red bell peppers (10½ oz/ 300g), *stems and seeds discarded, and flesh cut into 1¼–1½-inch/3–4cm pieces*

1 head of garlic, *skin on and halved crosswise*

3⅓ lb/1.5kg plum tomatoes, *peeled (optional) and roughly chopped*

1 cup/20g cilantro, *roughly chopped, plus 1 tbsp extra chopped cilantro to serve*

1 tbsp coriander seeds

4¼ oz/120g datterini or regular cherry tomatoes, *left whole*

4¼ oz/120g Greek feta, *roughly crumbled into large chunks*

¼ cup/25g pine nuts

1 tbsp rose harissa, *or ½ tbsp Tunisian harissa*

salt

1. Preheat the oven to 475°F.

2. Put 2 tablespoons of oil, the onions, jalapeños, peppers, and garlic into a large roasting pan about 13 x 10 inches/34 x 26cm in size and give everything a good stir. Roast for 25 minutes, stirring two or three times throughout, until softened and well charred.

3. Remove the garlic halves and use a small knife to remove the cloves, putting them back into the pan and discarding the papery skins. Add the plum tomatoes, cilantro, coriander seeds, and 1¾ teaspoons of salt and use the back of a large spoon to mash everything together, breaking apart the garlic and chiles a little. Return the pan to the oven for another 30–35 minutes, stirring two or three times throughout, or until the tomatoes have broken down and the mixture has thickened.

4. Remove the dish from the oven and set the oven broiler to high. Top with the datterini/cherry tomatoes and feta and drizzle with 1 tablespoon of oil. Broil for 10 minutes, or until the feta and datterini/cherry tomatoes have taken on some color.

5. Meanwhile, put the remaining 2 tablespoons of oil into a small frying pan on medium-high heat. Add the pine nuts and cook until golden, shaking the pan frequently, about 3 minutes. Add the harissa, stirring to combine, then remove from the heat.

6. To serve, spoon the harissa pine nuts over the top and sprinkle with the extra cilantro.

Make it your own:
- Use any soft herb you have on hand.
- Swap out the pine nuts for toasted almonds or walnuts.
- Veganize it: leave out the feta; it's just as tasty without.

Sticky sweet and sour plums and sausages

Prep time: *25 minutes*
Cook time: *1 hour 35 minutes*

Here we celebrate plums in all their beautiful red glory. As they cook, they gently break down to create a sweet/sour sauce for the sausages and potatoes. Paired with sticky pomegranate molasses and sour sumac, you can't really go wrong. Try to source pomegranate molasses from a Middle Eastern grocery store; it should be quite sharp and tangy and not overly sweet.

Serves 4

5 small red onions, *each cut into 6 wedges* *(1 lb 10 oz/750g)*

2 heads of garlic, *skin on and each halved crosswise*

3 russet potatoes *(1 lb 10 oz/750g), skin on and each quartered lengthwise*

½ cup/120ml olive oil

1 lb 10 oz/750g red plums *(about 10), halved and pitted (1 lb 5 oz/600g)*

3 rosemary sprigs

8 pork sausages *(1 lb 5 oz/600g)*

3 tbsp apple cider vinegar

¼ cup/90g pomegranate molasses

packed ¼ cup/50g light brown sugar

2 tbsp sumac

½ cup/10g parsley leaves, *with some stem attached*

salt and black pepper

1. Preheat the oven to 400°F.

2. Put the onions, garlic, potatoes, 5 tablespoons of oil, 7 tablespoons/100ml of water, 1½ teaspoons of salt, and a good grind of pepper into a large roasting pan roughly 16 x 12 inches/40 x 30cm in size. Toss everything together, then bake for 35 minutes, stirring halfway through, until the vegetables have softened and started to take on some color and the water has evaporated.

3. Add the plums (cut side up) and the rosemary, then nestle in the sausages. In a medium bowl, whisk together the vinegar, molasses, sugar, 2 tablespoons of water, 1½ tablespoons of sumac, 2 tablespoons of oil, ½ teaspoon of salt, and a good grind of pepper and pour this all over the mixture in the pan. Return to the oven for 40 minutes, carefully turning over the sausages halfway through. Turn the oven temperature up to 425°F and roast for 10 minutes more, or until everything is nicely browned, the plums have broken down, and the sauce is bubbling and sticky.

4. Toss together the parsley, the remaining 1½ teaspoons of sumac, and the remaining 1 tablespoon of oil and dot this all over the sausage mixture. Serve warm, directly from the pan.

Make it your own:
- Use any kind of sausages you like here: duck or chicken would work well, as would vegetarian sausages.
- Swap out the potatoes for sweet potatoes.

Fridge

Raid

Fridge raid

There's a universal sweet spot by the fridge, a familiar space in which we've all stood, door ajar and locked into a staring match with the fridge's contents. It's existing in that limbo between yourself and the next meal, waiting for inspiration to strike until . . . you see it. Eggs, begging to be pancakes. Rice, waiting to be fried. Chicken, wanting to be soup. As far as recipe-origin stories go, it's not that different at the OTK really. Sure, sometimes we'll go in with a fixed idea, a structured plan of how said dish should turn out, but this isn't always the case. Needless to say, we've all had to learn (the hard way, actually) that things don't always work out how we visualize them, diversions are a big part of the learning curve, and many accidents are, in fact, happy ones.

The recipes in this chapter, although born via fridge raid, all have one thing in common: they speak of comfort and familiarity. They are dishes that are relatable, things we know and love, and foods we grew up eating. With all the potential of comfort that this chapter has to offer, we tried hard to strike the right balance here between edgy and homey—dishes you'd want to dig into and eat, while also escaping predictability: a riff on mac 'n' cheese (p. 140), a Persian version of meatballs in tomato sauce (p. 156), or a very magical magical chicken and Parmesan soup (p. 143).

We want you to find comfort in this fridge raid chapter—echoes of familiarity in even the most unfamiliar of times—but also in other recipes dotted elsewhere in the book, as we put little spins on well-loved dishes that will hopefully find a place on your table.

Kale pesto strata with Gruyère and mustard

Prep time: *20 minutes*
Cook time: *1 hour 30 minutes*
Chilling time: *4 hours to overnight*

We're all about this strata, or savory bread pudding, as it's one to assemble a day ahead, ready to be popped into the oven when you're about an hour away from dinner. A lot less stress with little mess for when your guests are around, and a great one to have as a veggie main or as part of a brunch spread.

Serves 4–6

1 lb 2 oz/500g sourdough loaf, *ends discarded (but crusts intact) and loaf sliced into ¼-inch/½cm-thick slices*

2½ oz/75g kale, *stems discarded and leaves roughly torn*

2 cups/40g parsley, *roughly chopped*

¾ cup/15g oregano leaves

1 small Fresno chile, *roughly chopped (2 tbsp), seeded if you don't like heat*

1 large shallot, *roughly chopped into 6 wedges (½ cup/75g)*

2 garlic cloves, *roughly chopped*

9 tbsp/135ml olive oil, *plus extra for greasing*

½ cup/50g coarsely grated Parmesan

½ cup/60g coarsely grated Gruyère

3 large eggs

3 large egg yolks

3 cups/700ml whole milk

1¼ cups/300ml heavy cream

1½ tbsp Dijon mustard

1½ tbsp roughly chopped capers

1½ tbsp apple cider vinegar

salt and black pepper

1. Preheat the oven to 350°F. Spread the bread on two baking sheets and bake for 10 minutes, or until lightly toasted. Set aside to cool.

2. Grease a 12 x 8 inch/30 x 20cm baking dish that is at least 2½ inches/6cm deep.

3. Make the pesto. Put the kale, parsley, oregano, chile, shallot, and garlic into a food processor and pulse until finely chopped. Add 6 tablespoons/90ml of oil, ¾ teaspoon salt and a good grind of pepper, and pulse to a coarse paste. Measure out ⅓ cup/75g of the mixture and set aside.

4. Use the rest of the kale mixture to generously coat both sides of the toasted bread slices. Layer the bread in the baking dish at an angle, sprinkling both cheeses in between as you go, so that the pieces overlap a little.

5. In a medium bowl, whisk together the eggs, yolks, milk, cream, mustard, ¾ teaspoon of salt, and a good grind of pepper. Pour this over the bread, cover the dish with a piece of parchment paper, then weigh everything down with another, heavy baking dish. Refrigerate for at least 4 hours or preferably overnight.

6. Remove the strata from the fridge about 1 hour before baking, removing the weight and parchment. Cover tightly with foil.

7. Preheat the oven to 400°F. Bake for 30 minutes, then remove the foil and bake for 25 minutes more, or until deeply golden and bubbling. Let cool for at least 15 minutes before serving.

8. Combine the reserved pesto with the capers, vinegar, and the remaining 3 tablespoons of oil and spoon this all over the strata to serve.

Make it your own:

- Swap out the kale for spinach and the herbs for whatever you have on hand.
- Use a mixture of different cheeses—cheddar and pecorino would work well here!

_____

_____

_____

M.E. mac 'n' cheese with za'atar pesto

Prep time: *25 minutes*
Cook time: *30 minutes*

This recipe is a Middle Eastern take on a mac 'n' cheese thanks to the addition of cumin, an herbaceous za'atar pesto, and crispy fried onions. Cooking the macaroni in the milk, as we do here, bypasses having to make a béchamel. The starches are released into the soon-to-be-cheesy sauce, making it velvety and rich without the need for the more traditional flour-butter roux.

To make the crispy onions, finely slice a couple of onions into thin rounds and toss with 2 tablespoons of cornstarch. Fry in hot vegetable oil in about three batches, for 4 minutes per batch, or until golden.

Serves 4–6

MAC 'N' CHEESE

10½ oz/300g dried cavatappi or fusilli pasta

2½–3 cups/600–700ml whole milk

5 tbsp/65g unsalted butter, *cut into roughly 1¼-inch/3cm cubes*

3 garlic cloves, *minced*

⅛ tsp ground turmeric

1½ tsp cumin seeds, *toasted and roughly crushed with a mortar and pestle*

5 tbsp/75ml heavy cream

1⅓ cups/150g coarsely grated mature cheddar

6⅓ oz/180g Greek feta, *roughly crumbled*

salt and black pepper

½ cup/45g crispy onions or shallots, *store-bought or homemade (see intro)*

ZA'ATAR PESTO

1 large lemon

3 tbsp za'atar

1 cup/20g cilantro, *chopped*

1 garlic clove, *chopped*

⅓ cup/40g pine nuts, *lightly toasted*

6 tbsp/90ml olive oil

Get ahead:

– Make the mac 'n' cheese ahead of time if you like, adding a splash of water to thin out when reheating.

Make it your own:

– Play with different cheeses and spices.
– Use different pasta shapes like macaroni, adjusting liquid levels as necessary.

---

1. Put the pasta, 2½ cups/600ml of milk, 1½ cups/360ml of water, the butter, garlic, turmeric, 1 teaspoon of salt, and a good grind of pepper into a large sauté pan on medium-high heat. Bring to a simmer, then turn the heat down to medium and cook, stirring occasionally, for 10–14 minutes, or until the pasta is al dente and the sauce has thickened from the pasta starches (it will still be quite saucy). If using cavatappi, you might need to add the extra ½ cup/100ml of milk at this stage depending on how saucy you like your mac 'n' cheese. Turn the heat down to low and stir in the cumin, cream, and both cheeses until the cheddar is nicely melted.

2. While the pasta is cooking, make the pesto. Finely grate the lemon to get 1½ teaspoons of zest. Then use a small, sharp knife to peel and segment the lemon and roughly chop the segments. Place in a bowl with the lemon zest and set aside. Put the za'atar, cilantro, garlic, pine nuts, ⅛ teaspoon of salt, a good grind of pepper, and half the oil into a food processor and pulse a few times until you have a coarse paste. Add to the chopped lemon in the bowl and stir in the remaining oil.

3. Transfer the mac 'n' cheese to a large serving platter with a lip or a shallow bowl, dot all over with the pesto, then top with the crispy onions.

Magical chicken and Parmesan soup with pappardelle

Prep time: *15 minutes*
Cook time: *2 hours 25 minutes*

There's an undivided, universal power to chicken soup that translates across all cultures and borders. This broth is basically liquid magic, but our guess is the Parmesan rind might have something to do with it.

Serves 4

1 whole chicken *(3 lb/1.4kg)*

1 head of garlic, *skin on and halved crosswise, plus 4 extra peeled cloves, minced*

1 onion, *cut into 4 wedges*

2 tbsp olive oil

2 carrots, *peeled and roughly cut into ½-inch/1½cm cubes (1¾ cups/220g)*

3 sticks of celery, *sliced at an angle into roughly ½-inch/1cm-thick slices (2 cups/200g)*

3 bay leaves

1½ tbsp finely chopped thyme leaves

1 Parmesan wedge, *2¼ oz/60g finely grated (½ cup)and rind reserved*

5 plum tomatoes, *coarsely grated (p. 88) and skins discarded (1¾ cups/320g)*

2 tsp tomato paste

6⅓ oz/180g dried pappardelle nests

¾ cup/15g basil leaves, *finely sliced*

1 small Fresno chile, *seeded and finely chopped (1 tbsp)*

salt and black pepper

1. Put the chicken, head of garlic, onion, 8½ cups/2 liters of water, and 2¼ teaspoons of salt into a large saucepan, for which you have a lid, and bring to a boil. Lower to a simmer on medium-low heat and cook, covered, for 80 minutes, or until the chicken is tender.

2. Remove the chicken and, when cool, shred the meat into large pieces, discarding the skin, bones, and cartilage. Set aside.

3. Strain the stock through a sieve placed over a medium saucepan, discarding the solids. You will need 7 cups/1.7 liters, so save any extra for another use.

4. Heat the oil in a large saucepan on medium-high heat. Add the carrots and celery and cook for 4 minutes, until slightly softened. Add the minced garlic, bay leaves, thyme, and Parmesan rind and cook for 30 seconds more. Add the grated tomatoes and tomato paste and cook for another 3 minutes, or until the tomatoes cook down slightly. Pour in the 7 cups/1.7 liters of stock, add ½ teaspoon salt and a generous grind of pepper, and bring to a boil. Lower the heat to medium and cook for 15 minutes, or until the vegetables have softened.

5. Transfer 2 to 3 ladlefuls of soup, about 50/50 liquid to solids (avoiding the bay leaves and rind), to a blender, blitzing until completely smooth. Stir the blitzed soup back into the saucepan and return to medium-high heat. Add the pappardelle, the shredded chicken, and a good grind of pepper and cook for 15 minutes, until the pasta is al dente. Discard the bay leaves and the Parmesan rind.

6. Divide the soup among four bowls and top with the basil and chile, a good grind of pepper, and a sprinkling of grated Parmesan.

Make it your own:
- Swap out the pappardelle for other pasta shapes! We also like mafalda pasta.
- Leave out the chile for a kid-friendly version.

_____

_____

_____

Celebration rice with lamb, chicken, and garlic yogurt

Prep time: *15 minutes*
Cook time: *2 hours 20 minutes*
Soaking time: *1 hour +*

This warming spiced rice is a definite show-stopper, the kind of meal you'd make for a special occasion. We toyed over including this recipe in the book, laborious as it is, but, in all honesty, Noor wouldn't have it any other way. Rice, she believes, deserves to be prized and treasured—taking center stage at many a family table—and so, make this one as a weekend project, a feast of feasts, a real cause for celebration. Yes, it takes time, but here's a promise that it is oh-so-worth-it.

Serves 8

CHICKEN

1 whole chicken *(3 lb/1.4kg)*
2 cinnamon sticks
1 onion, *cut into 6 wedges (5¼ oz/150g)*
1 head of garlic, *skin on and halved crosswise*
1 tsp ground cumin
1 tsp ground cinnamon
2 tbsp olive oil
1½ tbsp lemon juice
¼ cup/5g parsley, *roughly chopped*
salt and black pepper

RICE

2 tbsp olive oil
3 tbsp unsalted butter
1 onion, *finely chopped (1 cup/150g)*
10½ oz/300g ground lamb
3 garlic cloves, *finely chopped*
1½ tsp ground cinnamon
1 tsp ground allspice
2 cups/400g basmati rice, *rinsed, soaked in cold water for at least 1 hour, and then drained*

1. Put the chicken into a large saucepan, for which you have a lid, along with the cinnamon sticks, onion, garlic, 8½ cups/ 2 liters of water, and 2 teaspoons of salt. Bring to a boil, then lower the heat to medium-low and simmer, covered, for 70 minutes, or until cooked through. Lift out the chicken and, when cool enough, tear into large bite-size chunks, discarding the skin and bones. Place the chicken in a bowl with the ground cumin and cinnamon and set aside. Strain the stock through a sieve set over a large bowl, discarding the solids. Measure out 3½ cups/ 850ml and keep warm (save the remainder for another use).

2. For the rice, put the oil and half the butter into a large saucepan, for which you have a lid, and place on medium-high heat. Add the onion and cook for 7 minutes, stirring often, until lightly golden. Add the lamb, garlic, and spices and cook for 2 minutes more, stirring often, until the lamb is no longer pink. Add the rice, 3 cups/700ml of the warm stock, 1¾ teaspoons of salt, and a good grind of pepper. Bring to a boil, then decrease the heat to low, cover with the lid, and cook for 15 minutes. Take off the heat and allow to sit, covered, for 15 minutes more. Add the remaining butter and set aside.

3. Meanwhile, make the yogurt sauce by whisking together the yogurt, garlic, ¾ teaspoon of salt, and the remaining ½ cup/150ml of warm stock in a medium bowl.

4. Put 2 tablespoons of oil into a large sauté pan on medium-high heat. Add the chicken pieces and cook for 5 minutes, to warm through. Remove from the heat, stir in the lemon juice and parsley, and set aside.

> **Get ahead:**
> – Cook the chicken the day before, refrigerating the flavorful stock and shredded chicken separately.

GARLIC YOGURT
3 cups/500g Greek yogurt
2 garlic cloves, *minced*

GARNISH
¼ cup/50g unsalted butter
¼ cup/30g blanched almonds
¼ cup/30g pine nuts
¾ tsp Aleppo chile, *or ½ tsp regular chile flakes*
¼ cup/5g parsley leaves
¼ cup/40g pomegranate seeds

5. Make the garnish by putting the butter into a small frying pan on medium-high heat. Add the almonds and cook for 3 minutes, stirring, until lightly colored. Add the pine nuts and cook for another 2 minutes, until golden. Remove from the heat and add the Aleppo chile.

6. Spread the rice over a large, round serving platter. Top with the chicken, then pour half the garlic yogurt over the top. Finish with the nuts and butter, followed by the parsley and pomegranate seeds. Serve the remaining yogurt alongside.

Make it your own:

– Swap out the lamb for ground beef, or a mixture of the two, if you wish. The cinnamon rice is a treat on its own, so skip out on everything else if you want to, and eat this with some veggies and a spoonful of yogurt.

_____

_____

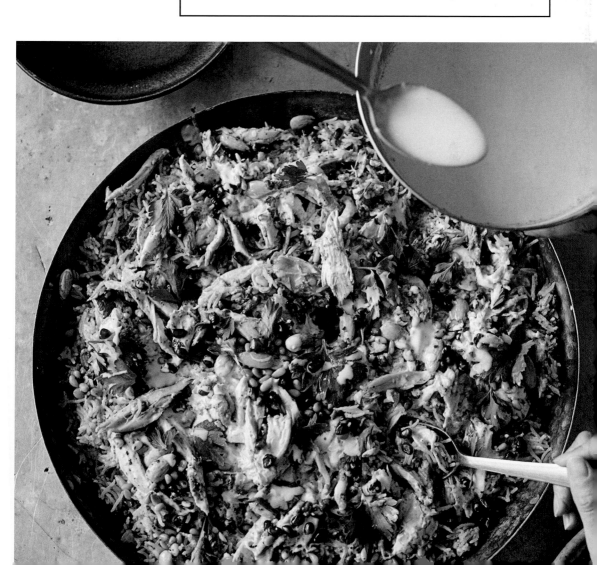

Smoky, creamy pasta with burnt eggplant and tahini

Prep time: *15 minutes*
Cook time: *1 hour 10 minutes*

Burnt eggplants, charred vegetables, and nutty tahini are what give this dish a real depth and smokiness, resulting in creamy, vegan pasta made without cream, cheese, butter, or any of the usual suspects. If you don't have a grill pan, char the vegetables in the oven instead.

Serves 4

5 eggplants *(2¾ lb/1.25kg),*
2 cut into 1¼–1½-inch/
3–4cm cubes and 3 left whole

⅔ cup/160ml olive oil

1 onion, *cut into 6 wedges*
(5¼ oz/150g)

2 small vine tomatoes, *left*
whole (7 oz/200g)

1 small Fresno chile
(⅓ oz/10g), left whole

3 tbsp tomato paste

1 tsp paprika

7 garlic cloves, *minced*

rounded ¼ cup/80g tahini

1 tbsp lemon juice

10½ oz/300g dried pasta
shells *(conchiglie rigate)*

½ cup/10g parsley, *roughly*
chopped

salt and black pepper

> *Get ahead:*
> – Make the burnt eggplant base up to 3 days ahead, reheating it with the pasta water on the day you want to serve it.
> – Double or triple the tahini sauce and keep a jar of it in your fridge. Thin it out with a splash of water if needed. Drizzle it over basically everything.

1. Preheat the oven to 450°F. Put the eggplant cubes on a large, parchment-lined baking sheet and toss with 3 tablespoons of oil, ½ teaspoon of salt and a good grind of pepper. Roast for 30 minutes, stirring halfway through, until deeply browned and softened.

2. Grill your vegetables. Prick the whole eggplants all over with a fork and ventilate your kitchen well. Place a well-greased grill pan on high heat and, once smoking, add the eggplants and cook, turning as necessary, for 35 minutes, or until well charred all over. Set aside to cool slightly. Toss the onion, tomatoes, and chile together in a bowl with a tablespoon of oil and cook in the same pan for 10 minutes, turning as necessary, until very well charred and softened. Transfer to a bowl, discarding the chile stem. Once cool enough to handle, peel and discard the skin and stems of the charred eggplants (it's okay if there is still some skin attached) and add the flesh to the bowl of charred vegetables. You should have roughly 11¼ oz/320g of eggplant flesh.

3. Meanwhile, put the tomato paste, paprika, three-quarters of the garlic, and 4 tablespoons of oil into a small saucepan on medium heat and cook, stirring occasionally, until the garlic is fragrant and the tomato paste has turned dark red, about 5 minutes. Transfer this and the grilled vegetables to a food processor, along with ¾ teaspoon of salt and a good grind of pepper, and blitz until completely smooth. Transfer to a large sauté pan and set aside. This is your sauce base.

4. In a small bowl, whisk together the tahini, the remaining garlic, the lemon juice, 5 tablespoons/70ml of water and a pinch of salt until smooth.

5. Cook the pasta in plenty of salted boiling water for 8 minutes, or until al dente. Reserve 1 cup plus 2 tablespoons/275ml pasta water, then drain the pasta well.

6. Add the reserved pasta water and half the roasted eggplant to the sauce base and heat through on medium-high heat. Add the drained pasta and stir to warm through, about 2 minutes.

7. Toss the remaining roasted eggplant with the parsley and the last 3 tablespoons of oil.

8. Transfer the pasta to a large serving platter with a lip, drizzle with a good amount of the tahini sauce, then spoon the eggplant and parsley mixture over the top. Serve the extra tahini sauce alongside.

Make it your own:

- Try the eggplant sauce mixed with bulgur wheat, couscous, or rice.
- Repurpose the eggplant sauce: thin it out with water to have as a soup with tahini and toasted croutons, or leave out the water entirely, to have as a dip with flatbreads.

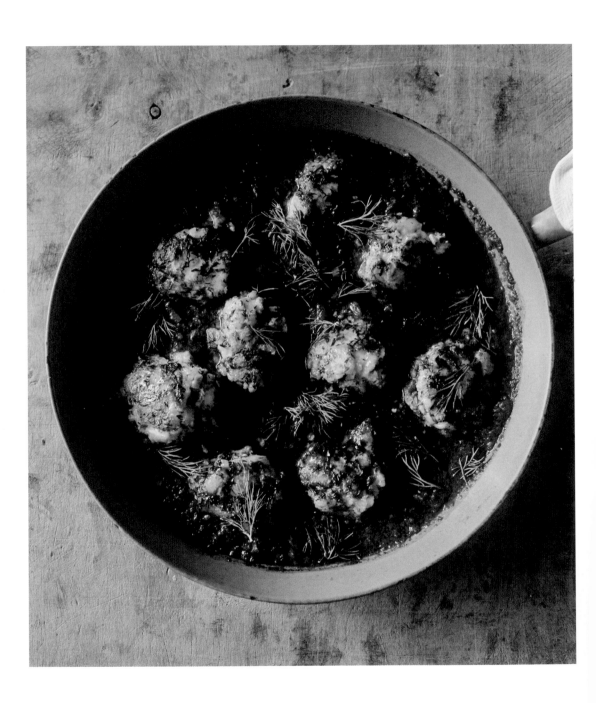

Fish koftas in ancho chile and tomato sauce

Prep time: *30 minutes*
Cook time: *1 hour 10 minutes*

The secret to these koftas is in the sauce: smoky ancho chile, caraway, and cumin adding depth to the whole experience. Tame the spicy kick here by serving with fluffy white rice and some cooling yogurt.

Serves 4

KOFTAS

1 lb 2 oz/500g firm sustainable white fish *(such as cod), boneless and skinless*

6 green onions, *finely sliced (¾ cup/60g)*

½ cup/10g dill, *chopped, plus extra leaves to serve*

1 small serrano chile, *seeded and finely chopped*

1½ tsp grated lemon zest

1 large egg, *beaten*

¼ cup/30g panko breadcrumbs

3 tbsp olive oil

TOMATO SAUCE

½ oz/15g dried ancho chiles *(about 1½ chiles), stems removed*

2 tsp caraway seeds, *toasted and roughly crushed*

1 tbsp cumin seeds, *toasted and roughly crushed*

6 garlic cloves, *peeled*

1 onion, *roughly chopped*

4 tbsp/60ml olive oil

1 small serrano chile, *halved lengthwise*

1 tbsp tomato paste

3–4 plum tomatoes *(14 oz/400g), roughly grated (p. 88) and skins discarded*

1¼ cups/300ml chicken or vegetable stock

2 tsp sugar

1¼ cups/25g cilantro, *roughly chopped*

salt and black pepper

1. First, make the sauce. Put the ancho chiles into a small bowl and cover with plenty of boiling water. Let soften for 20 minutes, then drain, discarding the liquid. Roughly chop the chiles, then put them into a food processor along with two-thirds of the caraway and cumin, all the garlic, the onion, and 2 tablespoons of oil, and blitz to a coarse paste.

2. Heat the remaining 2 tablespoons of oil in a large sauté pan on medium-high heat. Add the ancho paste, serrano chile, and tomato paste and cook for 7 minutes, stirring often, until softened and fragrant. Add the grated tomatoes, stock, ¾ cup plus 2 tablespoons/200ml water, the sugar, half the cilantro, 1¼ teaspoons of salt, and a good grind of pepper and bring to a boil. Lower the heat to medium and simmer for 15 minutes. Keep warm on low heat until needed.

3. Meanwhile, make the koftas. Finely chop the fish into ¼–½-inch/½–1cm pieces. Put them into a large bowl along with the green onions, dill, chile, lemon zest, egg, panko breadcrumbs, the remaining cilantro, the remaining caraway and cumin, 1 teaspoon of salt, and a good grind of pepper and mix well to combine. Form into 12 round fish cakes, roughly 2½–3 inches/6–7cm in diameter and about 2 oz/55g in weight. Make sure to press and compact them well, so they stay together when frying.

4. Heat 1½ tablespoons of oil in a large frying pan on medium-high heat. Add half the koftas and fry for 2½ minutes per side, until golden. Transfer to a plate, then repeat with the remaining oil and koftas.

5. Bring the sauce to a simmer on medium-high heat. Add the koftas, then turn the heat to medium-low and cook for 10 minutes, to cook through. Let sit for about 5 minutes, then top with the extra dill leaves and serve directly from the pan.

Get ahead:
– Make the sauce up to 2 days in advance—it will only intensify as it sits.
– Prepare the kofta mix the day ahead, shaping and pan-frying the day you intend to cook them.

Smoky marinated feta

Prep time: *10 minutes*
Cook time: *15 minutes*

Yotam admits to keeping a jar of this feta in his fridge lately, coming back to it for breakfast (on toast with sliced avocado), supper (over baked potato with an egg and chopped salad), or a sneaky pre-bed snack (with a glass of wine . . . or three). Can we blame him? Not really.

Serves 4–6, as a snack

10 garlic cloves, *peeled*

1–2 lemons: *finely shave the peel to get 8 strips and then juice to get ½ tbsp*

4 bay leaves

2½ tsp chipotle chile flakes

1½ tsp paprika

1 cup/240ml olive oil

1 tsp flaked sea salt

9½ oz/270g Greek feta *(about 1½ blocks), cut into ¾-inch/2cm cubes*

1. Place a small sauté pan on medium-high heat. Once very hot, add the garlic and cook for about 3–4 minutes, turning halfway through, until charred on the outside. Add the lemon strips and bay leaves and cook for 90 seconds more, then add the chipotle chile flakes and cook, stirring continuously, until well toasted and fragrant, about 20 seconds. Remove from the heat and add the paprika, oil, and salt, stirring to combine. Let cool completely.

2. Stir in the feta, then transfer to a bowl or glass jar with a lid and let marinate for at least 30 minutes, at room temperature if eating in the next couple hours or refrigerated (covered) if having it later.

3. If refrigerating, take the feta out of the fridge about 1 hour or so before you want to serve it, for the oil to come back up to room temperature. Add the lemon juice just before serving.

> *Get ahead:*
> – This will keep in the fridge for up to 1 week in a sealed container. Bring it back up to room temp before spooning it over your favorite things.

> *Make it your own:*
> – Add other spices or swap out the chipotle for other types of crushed dried chile.
> – Use the chile oil instead of cheese for sprinkling over beans, or to spoon over eggs and/or veggies.

Mediterranean-style fried rice with anchovy lemon dressing

Prep time: *20 minutes*
Cook time: *25 minutes*

This Mediterranean take on fried rice has all the crispy and salty bits as well as the very best bit: the crispy tahdig layer at the bottom of the pan. Tahdig is the Persian word referring to the bottom of the pot, where the rice forms a crunchy golden layer of crispy decadence. Like the bottom of an Asian claypot rice or the socarrat in Spanish paella, this scorched rice is the part we look forward to the most.

Serves 2

¼ cup/60ml olive oil

1 green bell pepper, *stem and seeds discarded and flesh cut roughly into 1¼-inch/3cm cubes (1 cup/150g)*

6 small garlic cloves, *peeled*

1 small Fresno chile, *halved lengthwise*

4 green onions, *white and green parts separated, each cut into 1¼-inch/3cm lengths (mounded ¾ cup/50g)*

¼ cup/5g thyme leaves, *with their soft sprigs*

1¾ cups/350g cooked basmati rice

2 large eggs

ANCHOVY DRESSING

½ oz/15g anchovies in oil *(about 5), drained and finely chopped*

2 garlic cloves, *minced*

½ tsp cumin seeds, *roughly crushed with a mortar and pestle*

2 tbsp olive oil

1 lemon: *finely shave the peel to get 6 strips and then juice to get 1½ tbsp*

1 tbsp roughly chopped parsley leaves

salt and black pepper

1. Make the anchovy dressing by putting the anchovies, garlic, cumin, oil, and a good grind of pepper into a small saucepan on medium heat. As soon as the mixture starts to bubble, remove it from the heat and add the lemon juice. Set aside to cool, then stir in the parsley.

2. Put 1 tablespoon of oil into a large frying pan, for which you have a lid, on medium-high heat. Add the green pepper pieces and cook for 3 minutes, stirring occasionally, until nicely colored and softened. Add 2 more tablespoons of oil, the garlic, red chile, and the white parts of the green onions and cook for 90 seconds more, until they've also taken on some color. Now add the green parts of the green onions, the thyme, and lemon peel and cook for another 30 seconds, then add the rice, ¼ teaspoon of salt, and a good grind of pepper. Stir frequently, breaking apart any clumps with a spoon, and cook for 3 minutes to take on a little color.

3. Use a spoon to create two wells in the rice mixture, exposing the bottom of the pan. Add 1½ teaspoons of oil to each well, then crack an egg into both and turn the heat down to medium. Sprinkle lightly with salt and pepper, cover with the lid, and cook for about 4–5 minutes, or until the whites are set, the yolks are still runny, and the bottom of the rice is nice and crispy. Drizzle all over with the anchovy dressing and serve right away.

Make it your own:
- Lose the fish: replace the anchovies with salty, briny capers.
- Use up whatever leftover rice you have, jasmine rice or brown, or even a mixture of both!
- Try it with orzo or giant couscous instead of the rice.

_____

_____

_____

Tomato and zucchini loaf with spiced tomato chutney

Prep time: *35 minutes*
Cook time: *2 hours 30 minutes*

Not quite veggie loaf and not quite bread, this savory loaf is perfect to serve at any and every mealtime. The chutney really is quite special and is what sets this loaf apart, so feel free to double the recipe and use it for other purposes—to eat with cheese and crackers, or to spread on a juicy burger.

Serves 4–6

2 small zucchini
(12¼ oz/350g), roughly grated
2¼ cups/275g all-purpose flour
2 tsp baking powder
½ tsp baking soda
1½ tsp garam masala
1 tsp sugar
2 large eggs
5 tbsp/75ml olive oil
¼ cup/70g Greek yogurt
1⅓ cups/150g coarsely grated mature cheddar
1¼ cups/25g cilantro, *roughly chopped*
2½ oz/75g mixed (red and yellow) cherry tomatoes, *halved*

TOMATO CHUTNEY
5 tbsp/75ml olive oil
6 garlic cloves, *minced*
1½ oz/45g fresh ginger, *peeled and finely grated*
2 small Fresno chiles, *finely chopped, seeds and all (3 tbsp)*
1½ tbsp tomato paste
½ tsp ground turmeric
2 tsp garam masala
1½ tbsp sugar
1 lb 10 oz/750g tomatoes, *cored and finely chopped, seeds and all*
salt and black pepper

1. Make the chutney by putting 4 tablespoons of the oil into a large sauté pan on medium-high heat. Once the oil is hot, add the garlic, ginger, and chiles and cook for 2 minutes, stirring occasionally, until fragrant. Add the tomato paste, turmeric, garam masala, and sugar and cook for 1 minute more, then add the chopped tomatoes, 1 teaspoon of salt, and a good grind of pepper. Bring to a simmer, then turn the heat down to medium and cook for 45 minutes, stirring often, until the tomatoes have completely broken down and the mixture is nice and thick. Measure out ½ cup/150g of the chutney and set aside to cool.

2. Preheat the oven to 400°F. Line a 9 x 5 inch/900g loaf pan with a piece of parchment paper large enough to cover the bottom and sides.

3. Meanwhile, put the zucchini and ½ teaspoon of salt into a bowl and mix to combine. Set aside for 20 minutes, then transfer the mixture to a clean kitchen towel and wring out as much liquid as possible. You want about 1 cup/180g of strained zucchini.

4. Put the flour, baking powder, baking soda, garam masala, sugar, and 1 teaspoon of salt into a large bowl and mix to combine. In a separate bowl, whisk together the eggs, 4 tablespoons of oil, and yogurt, then stir in the cheddar and cilantro. Add this, the zucchini, and the measured ½ cup/150g of tomato chutney to the flour bowl and mix gently to combine. Transfer the mixture to the prepared loaf pan, smoothing out the top to evenly distribute.

5. Arrange the halved cherry tomatoes on top, cut side up, gently pushing them into the surface. Drizzle with another 1 tablespoon of oil and bake for 40 minutes. Remove from the oven and lower the temperature to 375°F. Cover with foil, then return to the oven and bake for 45 minutes more, or until a skewer inserted into the center comes out clean. Set aside to cool in the pan for at least 30 minutes, or longer if time allows.

6. Slice the loaf as you need. Stir the remaining 1 tablespoon of oil into the chutney and serve in a bowl alongside, to spread. If not serving the same day, store well wrapped—it will keep for up to 2 days.

Make it your own:
- Use up other spices in the chutney, such as cumin and coriander or cinnamon and allspice.
- Use other oozy cheeses, such as Gruyère.

_____

_____

_____

Get ahead:
- Make the chutney well in advance and keep in a sealed jar in the fridge for up to 1 week.

Rice koofteh in spiced tomato sauce

Prep time: *30 minutes*
Cook time: *1 hour 30 minutes*

This is meatballs in tomato sauce, but with a very Persian twist. Yellow split peas are also often thrown into the mix, but we used a bit of chickpea (gram) flour instead. The sauce thickens as it sits, so add a splash more water if you're getting ahead. Eat these koofteh with some veggies and a spoonful of yogurt, if you like.

Serves 6

1¼ cups/250g basmati rice, *rinsed until the water runs clear and drained well*

1 lb 2 oz/500g ground beef or lamb *(15% fat), or a mixture of both*

½ onion, *roughly grated on a box grater (⅓ cup/60g)*

2 cups/40g parsley, *finely chopped, plus extra leaves to serve*

2 cups/40g cilantro, *finely chopped*

2 cups/40g dill, *finely chopped, plus extra leaves to serve*

1 large egg

⅓ cup/30g chickpea (gram) flour, *or rice flour*

½ tsp chile flakes

1½ tsp ground cumin

1½ tsp ground cinnamon

½ tsp ground turmeric

salt and black pepper

TOMATO SAUCE

3 tbsp olive oil, *plus extra for shaping the koofteh*

1 large onion, *finely chopped*

6 garlic cloves, *minced*

12¼ oz/350g tomatoes *(about 3), finely chopped*

5 tbsp/70g tomato paste

2¼ oz/60g soft dried apricots, *quartered (or 1½ tsp sugar)*

10 cardamom pods, *roughly bashed open with a mortar and pestle*

½ tsp chile flakes

1½ tsp ground cumin

1½ tsp ground coriander

1 tsp ground turmeric

1. Cook the rice for 10 minutes in plenty of boiling salted water, until just cooked through. Drain well in a sieve and set aside to cool (you should be left with about 3¼ cups/630g of cooked rice).

2. Make the koofteh by putting the ground beef or lamb, onion, herbs, egg, gram flour, and spices into a large bowl with 1¼ teaspoons of salt and a good grind of pepper. Add the cooled rice and use your hands to knead the mixture for about 5–6 minutes, until the rice grains are well crushed and the mixture is quite paste-like. This is a great arm workout, so switch arms halfway through.

3. Using well-oiled hands, shape the mixture into 12 large balls, roughly 4¼ oz/120g in weight. Refrigerate until ready to use.

4. Make the sauce by putting the oil into a large sauté pan, for which you have a lid, on medium-high heat. Add the onion and cook for 7 minutes, stirring occasionally, until golden. Add the garlic and cook for 30 seconds more, then add the tomatoes, tomato paste, apricots, and spices. Cook for 4 minutes, stirring occasionally, until the tomatoes have started to break down. Add 3½ cups/850ml of water, 1¼ teaspoons of salt, and a good grind of pepper, and bring to a gentle simmer. Add the koofteh, one at a time, then lower the heat to medium-low, cover with the lid, and let cook for 45 minutes, until the koofteh are cooked through and the sauce has reduced slightly (it will still be quite brothy, but will thicken as it sits).

5. Top with the extra parsley and dill leaves and serve warm, directly from the pan.

Make it your own:

– Use up whatever herbs you have on hand (tarragon and chives would be great here!) and whichever spices.
– Try this using other cooked grains instead, such as brown rice or bulgur wheat.

_____

_____

_____

Herby cabbage and potato gratin with Gruyère and ricotta

Prep time: *15 minutes*
Cook time: *2 hours
10 minutes*

Multiple layers of flavor make this gratin subtly special, the first being two types of garlic: sweet, sticky, and roasted, and then raw and pungent. The second being a multitude of herbs and cheeses in between layers of potato, shallots, and cabbage. It is as lovely to look at as it is to eat, and can be served as is, or alongside your protein of choice.

Serves 4

2 heads of garlic, *skin on and top fifth cut off to expose the cloves, plus 3 extra peeled cloves*

4 tbsp plus 1 tsp/65ml olive oil

1 lb/450g red potatoes *(about 4), skin on and sliced ⅛ inch/3mm thick*

2 shallots, *finely sliced on a mandolin or by hand (¾ cup/130g)*

2½ tsp smoked paprika

1 sweetheart/hispi cabbage or green cabbage, *base trimmed, thick stalks removed, and leaves separated (14 oz/400g)*

1 cup/20g basil, *finely chopped*

½ cup/10g tarragon leaves, *finely chopped*

1 cup/20g parsley, *finely chopped*

5 green onions, *finely sliced (mounded ¾ cup/50g)*

2 lemons: *finely grate the zest to get 1½ tbsp and then juice to get 1 tbsp*

¾ cup plus 1 tbsp/200g whole-milk ricotta

1⅓ cups/150g coarsely grated Gruyère

1 cup/240ml chicken or vegetable stock

salt and black pepper

1. Preheat the oven to 425°F.

2. Drizzle the garlic heads with 1 teaspoon of oil and sprinkle with a pinch of salt and pepper. Wrap each individually in foil and roast for 40 minutes, until softened and golden. Remove the foil and, when cool enough to handle, squeeze out the cloves, discarding the papery skins.

3. Meanwhile, prepare the rest of the vegetables. Combine the potatoes, shallots, and paprika in a bowl with 2 tablespoons of oil, ¾ teaspoon of salt, and plenty of pepper.

4. Toss the cabbage leaves together with 1 tablespoon of oil, ⅓ teaspoon of salt, and plenty of pepper.

5. Finely chop the three extra garlic cloves and mix together with all the herbs, the green onions, lemon zest, and the roasted garlic. Reserve a quarter of this mixture and set aside, to serve.

6. Assemble the gratin. Arrange a third of the cabbage leaves in the bottom of a 9 x 13-inch/23 x 33cm high-sided baking dish. Cover with half the potato mixture and a third of the herb mixture. Dot half of the ricotta and Gruyère randomly over the herbs. Repeat this once more, then top with a final layer of cabbage and the remaining third of the herb mixture.

7. Combine the stock, lemon juice, and ¼ teaspoon of salt and pour this evenly over the top, lifting some of the cabbage leaves up so the liquid sinks down. Cover tightly with foil and bake for 80 minutes, until the vegetables are soft. Drizzle with the remaining 1 tablespoon of oil and return to the oven, uncovered, for 15 minutes, to brown. Let cool for 10 minutes, then top with the reserved herb mixture.

Make it your own:
- Play with the cheeses!
- Play with the spices!

_____

_____

_____

_____

_____

Make it your own:

- Swap out the butternut squash for sweet potato or pumpkin.
- Alternatively, serve the butternut mash with flatbread instead of the pomlettes.
- Eat these pomlettes alongside the smooshed carrots (p. 68).

_____

_____

Spiced butternut mash with pancake omelettes (pomlettes)

Prep time: *25 minutes*
Cook time: *1 hour 10 minutes*

When we get asked what inspires us, our responses usually vary: home, friends, things we grew up eating, places we've visited, etc. Oftentimes, though, what inspires us at the OTK is each other— adding our own identities to something both new and familiar. These pancake-omelettes are the brainchild of Claudine, who struggled to find flour during lockdown and resourcefully used up the arrowroot in her cupboard, keeping these wonderfully gluten-free. Noor quickly renamed the pancake-omelettes "pomlettes," and found they were the perfect vehicle for this spiced butternut mash. Breakfast sorted.

Serves 4, generously

SPICED BUTTERNUT

- **1 lb 5 oz/600g butternut squash,** *peeled, seeded, and cut into roughly 1½-inch/4cm chunks*
- **7 tbsp/105ml olive oil**
- **1 small red onion,** *halved and thinly sliced (4¼ oz/120g)*
- **6 garlic cloves,** *minced*
- **1½ oz/40g fresh ginger,** *peeled and finely grated*
- **2 small serrano chiles,** *finely chopped, seeds and all*
- **2 tsp garam masala**
- **1 vine tomato,** *finely chopped (½ cup/100g)*
- **1 tsp cumin seeds**
- **20 fresh curry leaves** *(from 2 sprigs) (optional)*
- **1 tsp black mustard seeds**
- **salt**
- **½ cup/140g Greek yogurt,** *to serve*
- **1 lime,** *cut into 4 wedges, to serve*

PANCAKES

- **9 large eggs**
- **⅔ cup/90g arrowroot starch**
- **⅓ cup/90g Greek yogurt**
- **½ cup plus 2 tbsp/150ml whole milk**
- **½ tsp ground turmeric**
- **¼ cup/60ml olive oil**

1. Preheat the oven to 450°F.

2. Put the butternut squash, 1½ tablespoons of oil, ½ cup/ 120ml of water, and ½ teaspoon of salt into a 9 x 13 inch/23 x 33cm baking dish. Roast for 45 minutes, stirring halfway through, until nicely browned and the liquid has evaporated.

3. Meanwhile, put 2½ tablespoons of oil into a large sauté pan on medium-high heat. Once hot, cook the onion for 8–10 minutes, stirring occasionally, until softened and browned. Add the garlic, ginger, and chiles and cook for 3 minutes more, stirring often. Add the garam masala, tomato, and 3 tablespoons of water and cook for 4 minutes, until the tomato has broken down. Off the heat, add the roasted butternut squash and ½ teaspoon of salt and use a fork to roughly mash everything together. Keep warm until ready to serve.

4. Make the tempered oil by heating the remaining 3 table-spoons of oil in a small frying pan on medium-high heat. Add the cumin seeds and curry leaves and cook for 60–90 seconds, or until the leaves turn translucent.

Remove from the heat and add the mustard seeds.

5. Make the pancake mixture by putting everything except the oil into a food processor, along with 1 teaspoon of salt, and blitzing until smooth.

6. Heat 1 teaspoon of oil in a medium nonstick frying pan over medium-high heat. Ladle about ¼ cup/65g of the pancake batter into the pan, swirling to spread it around, and cook for 30 seconds on each side, or until nicely browned. Transfer to a plate and keep warm under a kitchen towel. Repeat with the remaining batter and oil to make 12 pancakes in total. Speed this up by using two frying pans.

7. When ready to serve, stir half the tempered oil into the butternut squash mixture and transfer to a bowl, spooning the remaining oil and solids on top. Arrange the pancakes on a large platter (they don't need to be neat). Put the yogurt into a bowl and nestle this and the butternut squash bowl around the pancakes with the lime wedges. Get everyone involved in building their own pancakes.

Make it your own:

- Go traditionally retro and add cooked peas and carrots, or shredded chicken.
- Swap out the nigella seeds for black sesame seeds if you like.

_____

_____

Beyond potato salad

Prep time: *25 minutes*
Cook time: *50 minutes*

This is a spin on the—very retro—salad Olivieh, a mayonnaise-based potato salad with many different variations, depending on whose household you're in. Some add shredded chicken, peas, or mashed carrots, some eliminate the egg. We kept this version veggie, using lots of lemon, herbs, and toasted seeds to jazz it up. It's a real use-up-what-you-have type of dish, suitable to take to picnics or to serve as a barbecue side.

Serves 6, as a side

1 lb 7 oz/650g yellow potatoes, *scrubbed clean, or a floury potato such as russet*

5 large eggs

6 tbsp/80g mayonnaise

¾ cup/220g Greek yogurt

3½ tbsp lemon juice

7 tbsp/105ml olive oil

1 oz/30g pickles, *thinly sliced into rounds*

½ cup/10g tarragon leaves, *roughly torn*

⅓ oz/10g chives, *sliced into ½-inch/1cm lengths*

1½ tsp coriander seeds, *roughly crushed with a mortar and pestle and toasted*

¾ tsp nigella seeds, *toasted*

¾ tsp sesame seeds, *toasted*

½ tsp Aleppo chile, *or ¼ tsp regular chile flakes*

salt and black pepper

1. Put the potatoes into a medium saucepan, for which you have a lid, and pour in enough water to cover by about 1½ inches/4cm. Season with 2 teaspoons of salt and bring to a simmer on medium-high heat. Turn the heat to medium, cover with the lid, and cook for 25 minutes, or until the potatoes are easily pierced with a fork. Drain and, when cool enough to handle, peel and discard the skins and roughly mash the potatoes in a large bowl to give you a lumpy mash.

2. Meanwhile, cook the eggs in boiling water for 8 minutes, or until just hard-boiled. Drain, peel, and discard the shells, then use a box grater to roughly grate the eggs, adding them to the potato bowl.

3. In a medium bowl, whisk together the mayonnaise, yogurt, 2½ tablespoons of lemon juice, 2 tablespoons of oil, 1 teaspoon of salt, and a generous grind of pepper. Add this to the potato mixture and mix well to combine. Transfer to a large serving plate, spreading to create a slight well in the center. Cover and refrigerate if not serving right away.

4. Mix together the pickles, tarragon, chives, the remaining 1 tablespoon of lemon juice and 5 tablespoons of oil, ⅛ teaspoon of salt, and a good grind of pepper. Spoon this all over the potato mixture.

5. Mix together all the toasted seeds and the chile and sprinkle this all over the top. Serve at room temperature or cold.

> *Get ahead:*
> – Make the day before and keep refrigerated, loosening it with a splash of water to serve, if needed.

Any grilled veg with mustard and Parmesan dressing

Prep time: *25 minutes*
Cook time: *1 hour*

Big plates of grilled vegetables never really go out of fashion. The key is to treat each vegetable individually, giving it the unique love and attention it deserves to make sure it shows up to the table looking its absolute best. We dress our grilled veggies in this sharp and cheesy dressing, but they do like a versatile wardrobe—so feel free to experiment with different vinaigrettes and sauces.

Serves 4

1 baked potato
(9 oz/250g), skin on and cut into ½-inch/1cm slices

14 oz/400g bunch of thick-stemmed asparagus, *woody ends trimmed (9 oz/250g)*

2 red bell peppers, *stems and seeds discarded and each pepper quartered (10½ oz/300g)*

2 red onions, *each cut into 4 x ½-inch/1½cm-thick rounds (8½ oz/240g)*

¼ cup/60ml olive oil, *plus extra for greasing*

6 small garlic cloves, *peeled*

2 baby gem lettuces, *core removed and leaves separated (5¼ oz/150g)*

¼ cup/5g parsley leaves, *with some stem attached*

½ tsp fennel seeds, *toasted and roughly crushed with a mortar and pestle*

salt and black pepper

MUSTARD PARMESAN DRESSING

2¼ tsp Dijon mustard

2 garlic cloves, *minced*

¼ cup/25g finely grated Parmesan

3 tbsp lemon juice

5 tbsp/75ml olive oil

1. Put the potato, asparagus, peppers, and onions into four separate bowls, and toss each with 1 tablespoon of oil and a pinch each of salt and pepper.

2. Make the dressing by putting all the ingredients into a bowl with ¼ teaspoon of salt and a good grind of pepper and whisking until combined.

3. Place a well-greased grill pan on high heat until smoking. Cook each of the vegetables separately, until nicely charred and softened. Cook the peppers for 15–20 minutes, the onions for 4 minutes on each side, the potatoes for 2 minutes on each side, the asparagus for 7 minutes in total and, lastly, the garlic cloves for 1 minute on each side. Set aside each of the grilled vegetables separately and, while they're still warm, spoon some of the dressing over the top to nicely coat them.

4. Toss the gem lettuce and parsley leaves together in any remaining dressing and transfer to a large plate. Arrange the grilled vegetables on the same plate and sprinkle with the fennel seeds to serve.

Make it your own:
– Play around with whatever vegetables you have on hand. Pre-cook those that need longer cooking, such as root vegetables.

_____

_____

_____

Cream of tomato soup with buttery onions and orecchiette

Prep time: *15 minutes*
Cook time: *1 hour 10 minutes*

This is basically Campbell's tomato soup but amplified, thanks to the added oomph of habanero chile and sweet buttery onions. This makes the soup a little more grown-up, so leave out the chile if you're making this kid-friendly or if you're not that into heat.

Serves 4

¼ cup/60g unsalted butter

6 tbsp/90ml olive oil

3 onions, *finely chopped (3⅔ cups/540g)*

2 large garlic cloves, *minced*

14 oz/400g sweet red cherry or datterini tomatoes

¼ cup/55g tomato paste

½ cup/10g basil leaves, *roughly torn*

1 dried habanero chile *(optional)*

2 cups/480ml vegetable or chicken stock *(or water)*

7 oz/200g dried orecchiette pasta

2 tbsp heavy cream *(or more, if you like)*

salt and black pepper

1. Put the butter, 3 tablespoons of oil, the onions, and 1 teaspoon of salt into a large sauté pan on medium heat and cook for 18–20 minutes, stirring often, until soft and deeply golden brown. Lower the heat if they get too brown.

2. Transfer two-thirds of the fried onions to a bowl and stir in the remaining 3 tablespoons of oil.

3. Return the pan with the remaining onions to medium heat, add the garlic, and fry for 2 minutes. Add the tomatoes, tomato paste, basil, habanero (if using), and 2 teaspoons of salt and fry for 7 minutes, stirring often. Increase the heat to medium-high, add the stock, 1¼ cups/300ml of water, and a good grind of pepper and bring to a simmer. Lower the heat to medium and cook for 12 minutes. Remove the habanero (if using) and squeeze to discard any liquid. Finely chop the habanero and stir into the bowl with the reserved fried onions.

4. Let the soup cool for 5–10 minutes, so it's not dangerously hot, then transfer to a blender and blitz until completely smooth.

5. Meanwhile, cook the orecchiette until al dente, then drain and divide among four bowls. Pour in the soup, then spoon the cream and the onion mixture over the top.

Make it your own:

- Leave out the habanero or swap out for another milder chile such as ancho or chipotle.
- Veganize it: leave out the cream and use extra olive oil instead of butter for the onions.
- Swap out the orecchiette for different pasta shapes or some cooked rice.

_____

_____

Gnocchi with sumac onions and brown butter pine nuts

Prep time: *25 minutes*
Cook time: *1 hour 35 minutes*

We use sumac onions liberally at the Test Kitchen, mostly because they lend just the right amount of acidity and sweetness (when cooked) or sharpness (when raw). The Middle East meets Italy here, and we can all vouch that sumac and gnocchi get along splendidly. If you don't have time to make gnocchi, then you can always use store-bought. Our very own Gitai says that he often uses jarred butter beans (lima beans) in place of the gnocchi as an even healthier option.

Serves 4, as a starter or light lunch

3 lb/1.4kg russet potatoes, *skin on and scrubbed clean, then pricked all over with a fork*

3 large egg yolks, *lightly beaten*

¾ cup plus 2 tbsp/110g all-purpose flour, *sifted*

2 tbsp olive oil, *plus extra for drizzling*

5 tbsp/70g unsalted butter

rounded ¼ cup/35g pine nuts

2 tbsp lemon juice

¼ cup/5g parsley leaves, *roughly chopped*

salt and black pepper

⅓ cup/80g crème fraîche, *to serve (optional)*

SUMAC ONIONS

2 tbsp olive oil

2 red onions, *halved and thinly sliced (12¾ oz/360g)*

½ tsp salt

4 garlic cloves, *minced*

4 tsp sumac

Get ahead:
– Make and boil the gnocchi a day in advance. Spread out on a well-oiled baking sheet and refrigerate until needed.

---

1. Preheat the oven to 450°F. Place the potatoes directly on the middle rack of your oven and bake for 45 minutes to 1 hour, or until cooked through.

2. Meanwhile, make the onions. Heat the oil in a large sauté pan on medium-high heat. Add the onions and ½ teaspoon of salt and cook for 12–15 minutes, stirring occasionally, until softened and browned. Add the garlic and cook for 2 minutes more, until fragrant. Stir in the sumac and remove from the heat. Transfer the mixture to a bowl and rinse out the pan.

3. While still hot (use a kitchen towel or gloves), slice open the potatoes and scoop out their insides, discarding the skins: you want about 1 lb 5 oz/600g. Use a potato ricer to finely mash the potato directly onto a clean work surface. Lightly spread the potato out so it's not all in one pile and sprinkle evenly with the egg yolks, followed by the flour and ½ teaspoon of salt. Use a pastry cutter or bench scraper to cut into the mixture, chopping repeatedly to evenly distribute everything. Use your fingers to gather everything together into a ball (don't knead the mixture at all). Transfer the mixture to a piping bag and set it aside.

4. Bring a large saucepan of well-salted water to a boil on medium-high heat. Snip off the end of your piping bag to create an opening about ¾ inch/2cm wide. Pipe 1¼-inch/3cm lengths of the gnocchi into the water (about 12 at a time), using a small sharp knife to release the dough, and cook for 1–2 minutes, or until the gnocchi float to the surface. Use a slotted spoon to transfer the gnocchi to a parchment-lined baking sheet, drizzling with a little oil to prevent them from sticking. Continue this way until you've cooked all the gnocchi, 4–5 batches.

5. Add 1 tablespoon of oil to the rinsed-out sauté pan from earlier and place on medium-high heat. Add a third of the gnocchi and cook for 4 minutes, until golden all over. Transfer to a parchment-lined baking sheet and continue in this way, adding ½ tablespoon of oil and a third of the gnocchi each time.

6. Melt the butter in the same pan on medium-high heat. Add the pine nuts, ½ teaspoon of salt, and a good grind of pepper and cook for 2 minutes, until golden. Turn the heat to low and add back all the gnocchi, sumac onions, lemon juice, and parsley, stirring gently to combine. Serve the crème fraîche alongside, if using.

Make it your own:

- Save time and use store-bought gnocchi, Gitai's butter beans suggestion (see headnote), or roasted diced potatoes.
- Double up on the sumac onions and fold them into mashed potatoes or pasta!

_____

_____

The

IS YOUR

Freezer

FRIEND

The freezer is your friend

The freezer is your most loyal friend—the kind of pal that'll take what you don't want, preserve it, and then give it back to you when you're good and ready (all the while never losing its cool). We're sometimes guilty of neglecting it, but then it's like digging through a treasure chest, filled to the brim with valuable finds and ice crystals. We have a little theory that much insight can be gained when having a rummage through a person's freezer. In typical "I'll show you mine if you show me yours" fashion, we had a quick Test Kitchen reveal.

What's in our freezers? Our answers vary . . . greatly. Chaya says Mauritian shrimp paste and fish fingers, her love for seafood very apparent. Yotam says sliced sourdough and pistachio ice cream (the good kind only, he emphasizes). Verena says dough, every single dough you can possibly think of, but mostly pie dough, ready to be baked at a moment's craving. Noor says nuts, fresh dates, and za'atar—there's no guessing which part of the world she's from. Ixta says Scotch bonnets and tortillas, ready to be turned into a taco when taco inspiration strikes. Gitai says berries and Parmesan rinds, a little bit fruity and a whole lotta funky. And, saving the best for last, Tara says frozen lasagne for the kids, and vodka for the adults (smart choices on both counts).

All in all, we decided that building a chapter on the various freezer identities out there would prove challenging, unique as they are. We therefore stuck to the universal freezer-favorites: frozen veggies like peas in our peas, tahini, and za'atar (p. 182); frozen pastry like filo in our curried cauliflower cheese filo pie (p. 179); frozen seafood like the frozen shrimp used in our cobb salad (p. 184); and frozen fruits like the mixed berries in our skillet berries, bread, and browned butter (p. 204). We know this just covers the bases, but here's hoping these recipes break the ice.

Curried cauliflower cheese filo pie

Prep time: *20 minutes*
Cook time: *1 hour 45 minutes*

Cauliflower cheese, but make it pie. This dish was once described as "molten-hot-cheese-lava" and we think that's pretty fitting for the ultimate comfort of comfort foods.

Serves 4, generously

1 large cauliflower,
  *trimmed and cut
  into bite-size florets
  (1 lb 9 oz/700g)*
2 tsp mild curry powder
3 tbsp olive oil
7 tbsp/100g unsalted
  butter, *half cut into roughly
  1¼-inch/3cm cubes and half
  melted*
½ cup plus 2 tbsp/75g
  all-purpose flour
2¾ cups plus 2 tbsp/675ml
  whole milk
2 garlic cloves, *minced*
1½ tbsp English
  mustard
1⅓ cups/150g coarsely
  grated mature cheddar
6 sheets of good-quality
  filo pastry *(we use feuilles
  de filo)*
salt and black pepper
1 tbsp roughly chopped
  parsley, *to serve*
1½ tsp lemon zest, *to serve*

1. Preheat the oven to 400°F. Line the bottom and sides of a 9-inch/23cm springform cake pan with parchment paper.

2. Put the cauliflower on a large, parchment-lined baking sheet and toss with the curry powder, half the oil, ½ teaspoon of salt, and a good grind of pepper. Roast for about 20 minutes, until cooked through and lightly colored. Set aside, and turn the oven temperature down to 375°F.

3. Meanwhile, make the béchamel. Put the cubed butter into a medium saucepan on medium-high heat and, once melted, whisk in the flour and cook for 1–2 minutes—it should start to smell nutty (like popcorn). Turn the heat down to medium and slowly add the milk a little at a time, whisking continuously to prevent any lumps, until incorporated and the sauce is smooth. Cook, whisking often, for about 7 minutes, until thickened slightly. Off the heat, stir in the garlic, mustard, cheese, and ¼ teaspoon of salt until the cheese has melted.

4. Keep the filo sheets under a damp kitchen towel to prevent them from drying out. In a bowl, combine the melted butter and the remaining 1½ tablespoons of oil and set aside.

5. Working with one sheet at a time, brush the exposed side of the filo with the butter mixture and drape it into your prepared pan (buttered side up), pushing it down gently to fit. Continue in this way with the next filo sheet, brushing it with butter and then laying it over the bottom sheet, rotating it slightly so the overhang drapes over the sides at a different angle. Do this with all six sheets.

6. Spoon half the béchamel into the base and top with the roasted cauliflower florets. Spoon in the remaining béchamel, then crimp up the overhang so that it creates a messy scrunched-up border around the edges, leaving the center of the pie exposed.

7. Brush the top of the filo border with the remaining butter mixture, then transfer the pan to a baking sheet and bake for 30 minutes.

8. Using a kitchen towel to help you, carefully release the outer circle of the springform pan and return the pie to the oven for another 20–25 minutes, or until the sides are nicely colored and everything is golden and bubbling. Let settle for 15 minutes.

9. Top the pie with the parsley and lemon zest and serve warm.

Make it your own:
- Try using shortcrust or puff pastry instead, being mindful of cooking times.
- Play with the cheese! Anything oozy and melty would work.
- Spice it up. Curry powder not enough? Add chile heat.

_____

_____

Peas, tahini, and za'atar

Prep time: *15 minutes*
Cook time: *10 minutes*

There are always bags of frozen peas in our freezers, ready to be tossed into salads or stews or blitzed into this easy pea dip. Serve with your choice of crudité or—our favorite—warm pita breads (p. 23).

Serves 4–6, as part of a mezze spread

4¼ cups/500g frozen peas, *defrosted*

¼ cup/65g tahini

2 cups/40g parsley, *roughly chopped*

1 cup/20g mint leaves

3 tbsp za'atar

2 lemons: *finely grate the zest to get 2 tsp and then juice to get 3 tbsp*

7 tbsp/105ml olive oil

1½ oz/40g breakfast radishes *(about 4), thinly sliced on a mandolin or by hand*

2 green onions, *thinly sliced at an angle (¼ cup/25g)*

salt and black pepper

1. Set aside ⅓ cup/50g of peas in a medium bowl for later.

2. Put the remaining peas, the tahini, herbs, 2 tablespoons of za'atar, the lemon zest and juice, 3 tablespoons of oil, 1¼ teaspoons of salt, and a good grind of pepper into a food processor and blitz into a smooth paste. Spread out on a large plate, using a spoon to create a shallow well in the center.

3. To the reserved peas add the radishes, green onions, 1 tablespoon of oil, ⅛ teaspoon of salt, and a good grind of pepper and toss to combine.

4. In a small bowl, whisk together the remaining 1 tablespoon of za'atar and the last 3 tablespoons of oil.

5. Drizzle the za'atar oil all over the pea dip, and top with the radish mixture.

Make it your own:

- Use any equivalent of soft herbs you have on hand (dill and tarragon would be great here).
- Swap out the tahini for Greek yogurt.

Cobb salad with mango and lime dressing

Prep time: *35 minutes*
Cook time: *40 minutes*

Cobb salads slide easily into the OTK ethos, as they're all about using up what you have to create something playful and vibrant. Here we invite you to the Cobb salad playground, using this recipe as a baseline. Dig through your cupboards, rummage through your fridge and freezer, use what you can and what you have, and then build from there—all the while keeping the spirit of abundance and fun.

Serves 4 as a main

6 slices of prosciutto
(2¼ oz/60g)

2 large eggs

¼ cup/60ml olive oil

12¼ oz/350g asparagus,
woody ends trimmed and spears cut crosswise into 3 (8 oz/220g)

1¾ cups/300g frozen corn kernels, *defrosted*

12 oz/340g frozen or fresh extra-large peeled shrimp, *defrosted if frozen and patted dry*

7 oz/200g datterini or regular cherry tomatoes, *halved*

1 large iceberg lettuce
(1 lb 2 oz/500g), chopped into bite-size pieces

¾ cup/15g cilantro leaves, *with some stem attached*

flesh of 1 large avocado, *thinly sliced*

1 small red onion *(3 oz/80g), very thinly sliced into rounds*

½ lime

salt and black pepper

MANGO LIME DRESSING

7 oz/200g frozen or fresh mango, *defrosted if frozen*

5 tbsp/75ml lime juice

¼ cup/60ml olive oil

2 anchovies in oil, *drained and roughly chopped*

¼ cup/5g cilantro, *finely chopped*

1 small Fresno chile, *seeded and finely chopped (1 tbsp/10g)*

1. Preheat the oven to 375°F.

2. Lay out the prosciutto on a large, parchment-lined baking sheet and bake for 15 minutes, until starting to crisp up. Let cool completely.

3. Meanwhile, boil the eggs for 7–8 minutes. Drain, run under cold water, then peel and cut each egg into quarters. Sprinkle lightly with salt and pepper and set aside.

4. Make the dressing. Put the mango, lime juice, oil, and anchovies into a food processor or blender and blitz until smooth. Transfer to a bowl and stir in the cilantro, chile, ⅓ teaspoon of salt, and a good grind of pepper.

5. Heat 1½ teaspoons of oil in a large sauté pan on medium-high heat. Add the asparagus, ¼ teaspoon of salt, and a good grind of pepper and cook for 4 minutes, to soften and char. Transfer to a baking sheet, then add 1 tablespoon of oil to the same pan along with the corn, ¼ teaspoon of salt, and a good grind of pepper and

cook, stirring occasionally, for 4 minutes, to char in places. Set aside, separately, and add another 1 tablespoon of oil to the pan, turning the heat to high. Once very hot, add half the shrimp, ¼ teaspoon of salt, and a good grind of pepper and cook for 3 minutes, until just cooked through and browned. Set aside, separately, and continue in the same way with another 1 tablespoon of oil, the remaining shrimp, and seasoning.

6. Toss the tomatoes together with a pinch of salt and pepper and 1½ teaspoons of oil.

7. In a large bowl, combine the lettuce, cilantro, a third of the dressing, ¼ teaspoon of salt, and a good grind of pepper. Spread out on a large serving platter. In separate piles, top the lettuce with the tomato, avocado, onion, corn, asparagus, eggs, prosciutto, and shrimp. Squeeze the lime half over the top, and drizzle with another third of the dressing, serving any extra alongside.

> **Get ahead:**
> – Make the dressing up to 2 days in advance.

Make it your own:

- Bring your Cobb salad to life by using up what you have.
- Vegify it: swap out the shrimp for tofu or seared mushrooms, replace the anchovies with capers, and leave out the prosciutto.

_____

_____

_____

Braised green beans with tomato, cardamom, and garlic

Prep time: *15 minutes*
Cook time: *55 minutes*

Slow-cooking green beans makes them wonderfully soft and comforting, despite not keeping their bright green hue. You can use frozen green beans as we do here, or fresh—depending on what you can find.

Serves 4, as a side

5¼ oz/150g datterini or
   regular cherry tomatoes
1 lb 3 oz/550g vine
   tomatoes *(about
   4–5), roughly chopped*
½ cup/120ml olive oil
1 onion, *halved and finely
   sliced (6⅓ oz/180g)*
10 garlic cloves, *thinly sliced*
8 whole cardamom pods,
   *lightly bashed open with a
   mortar and pestle*
1½ tsp ground cumin
½ tsp chile flakes
**1 lb/450g frozen green
   beans,** *defrosted and halved
   at an angle*
¾ cup/15g cilantro,
   *roughly chopped, plus extra
   whole leaves to serve*
salt and black pepper

1. Place a large sauté pan, for which you have a lid, on high heat. Once very hot, cook the datterini/cherry tomatoes for 5 minutes, to char all over. Transfer the tomatoes to a bowl and let the pan cool slightly.

2. Put the vine tomatoes into a food processor and blitz until puréed. Set aside until needed.

3. Return the pan to medium-high heat with 5 tablespoons of oil. Once the oil is hot, add the onion and cook for about 6 minutes, until softened and lightly browned. Add two-thirds of the garlic and all the cardamom and cook for 2 minutes more, until the garlic has taken on some color. Add the spices and cook for 30 seconds, then stir in the blitzed tomatoes, 1½ teaspoons of salt, and a good grind of pepper and cook for 7 minutes, stirring occasionally, until thickened. Add 1 cup/240ml of water and cook for 8 minutes more, then decrease the heat to medium, add the green beans, cover with the lid, and cook for 12 minutes. Give everything a stir, add the charred tomatoes, then replace the lid and cook for a final 8 minutes, until the beans are very soft. Stir in the chopped cilantro.

4. Meanwhile, put the remaining 3 tablespoons of oil and the remaining sliced garlic into a small frying pan and place it on medium heat. Cook for about 8 minutes, stirring occasionally, until the garlic is golden and crispy.

5. When ready to serve, transfer the green beans to a large shallow bowl or platter. Top with the whole cilantro leaves and spoon the fried garlic and its oil over the top. Serve at room temperature.

Get ahead:
– Make the whole dish, minus the crispy garlic and cilantro, the day before. The flavors will only intensify overnight.

Make it your own:

– Replace the frozen green beans with snow peas or okra.
– Serve this warm, with rice or braised meat.

_____

_____

_____

Vampire-slaying toum

Prep time: *20 minutes*
Cook time: *15 minutes*

Toum, which literally translates to "garlic" in Arabic, is a Levantine condiment made by whipping together raw garlic and oil with a good amount of lemon juice. It is potent enough to ward off even the most persistent of vampires and is most definitely not for the garlic averse among us. Use it sparingly, and if you find it *too* potent, swirl in some Greek yogurt, as we do in the following two recipes. Make sure to use a neutral-tasting oil here, such as vegetable oil, and not olive oil—it'll ensure the toum stays white and fluffy and won't detract from the intensely pungent garlic flavor. This recipe will most likely make more than you need, but toum is stable enough to have a long shelf life. Once made, store it in a sealed jar in the fridge; it'll keep for up to 4 weeks and goes really well with crispy potatoes, grilled meat (particularly when rich and fatty), and just about anything battered and fried. Lastly, toum loses its intensity the longer it sits, so for the more faint of heart, make this a few days in advance of when you need it.

Makes about 1½ cups/350g

3½ oz/100g garlic cloves, *peeled (about 2 heads)—make sure they are well dried*

1¼ cups/300ml vegetable oil *(9 oz/250g by weight), or another neutral-tasting oil*

5 tbsp/75ml lemon juice

salt

1. Halve the garlic cloves lengthwise and use a small, sharp knife to remove and discard the inner part (some will look green or similar to a white twig).

2. Transfer the cored-out garlic cloves to a food processor along with ¼ teaspoon of salt and 2 tablespoons of the oil. Blitz until very smooth and aerated, about 3 minutes, stopping to scrape down the bowl a couple times. With the machine still running, very slowly drizzle in about ¼ cup/60ml (a fifth) of the remaining oil, followed by 1 tablespoon of lemon juice. Continue in this way, alternating between oil and lemon juice and ending with the oil. Do this very slowly and steadily; you don't want the toum to split at all. You should be left with a white, fluffy, and homogenized mixture. Transfer to a sterilized, sealed jar and store refrigerated; it'll keep for up to 4 weeks.

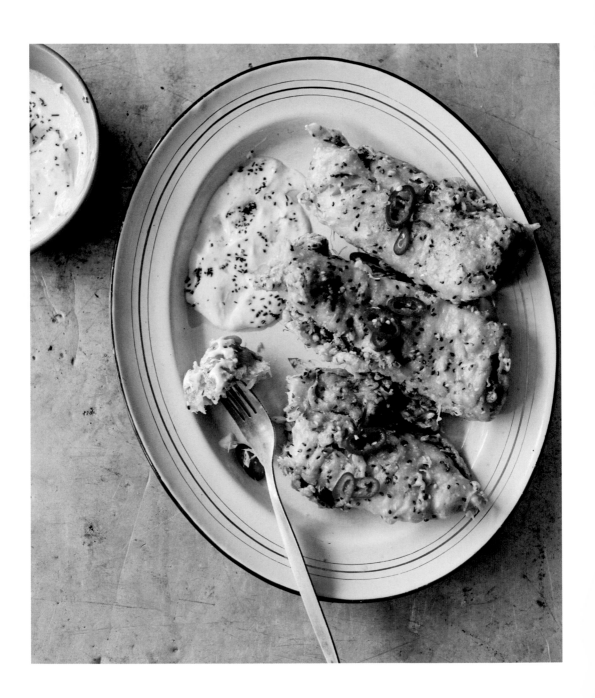

Buckwheat-battered fish with toum and pickled chiles

Prep time: *25 minutes*
Cook time: *50 minutes*

This gluten-free take on battered fish and mayo is a massive departure from anything traditional, but it works, with the buckwheat adding a lovely, nutty flavor to the batter. Swap the toum out with some store-bought mayonnaise or yogurt, if you like, although it really does make the dish super special.

Serves 4

1 small Fresno chile, *thinly sliced, seeds and all (1 tbsp)*

2 tbsp apple cider vinegar

scant ½ cup/100g toum *(p. 190)*

6 tbsp/100g Greek yogurt

½ tbsp finely chopped chives

1 tbsp olive oil

salt and black pepper

FISH

4 frozen fillets of sustainable white fish, *boneless and skinless, defrosted (1 lb 4 oz/560g)*

3 cups/700ml vegetable oil, *for deep-frying*

½ cup/55g cornstarch

7 tbsp/55g rice flour *(not the glutinous kind)*

7 tbsp/50g buckwheat flour

2 tbsp black and white sesame seeds, *toasted*

¾ cup/180ml sparkling water

1. Put the chiles, vinegar, and a tiny pinch of salt into a small bowl and set aside to pickle while you continue with the rest.

2. Pat dry the fish and season well with ½ teaspoon of salt and a good grind of pepper. Put the vegetable oil into a large, high-sided and nonstick sauté pan on medium-high heat and, while it's heating up, make the batter.

3. In a large bowl, whisk together the cornstarch, rice flour, buckwheat flour, sesame seeds, and ¾ teaspoon of salt, then slowly whisk in the sparkling water to make a thick, smooth, and pourable batter.

4. Drop a little bit of the batter into the oil to test it's hot enough. It should immediately start to sizzle and take on a little bit of color. Frying two at a time, dip a piece of fish into the batter until nicely coated and then drop it straight into the hot oil. Fry for 7 minutes, turning over halfway through, until lightly golden and cooked through. Transfer to a plate lined with paper towels and continue this way with the rest.

5. In a small bowl, combine the toum and the yogurt. Top with the chives and olive oil.

6. When ready to serve, place the fish on a large platter and spoon the pickled chiles over the top. Serve the toum mixture alongside.

Make it your own:
- We love this gluten-free batter so much, and can vouch that it works well with just about anything. If you're not into fish, then thinly sliced vegetables or tofu would work well here too.
- Swap out the rice or buckwheat flour for the equivalent amount of all-purpose flour.

194

Fava bean and herb salad with toum

Prep time: *25 minutes*
Cook time: *20 minutes*

This fresh, sharp salad and toum-yogurt makes a lovely side to heartier dishes and fatty meats.

Serves 4, as a side

1 large lemon

3 cups/350g frozen
  or fresh shelled fava
  beans, *defrosted if frozen
  and skins removed*

2 baby gem lettuces,
  *core removed and leaves
  separated*

½ cup/10g tarragon leaves

½ cup/10g mint leaves

½ cup/10g dill leaves

3 tbsp olive oil

scant ½ cup/100g toum
  (p. 190)

6 tbsp/100g Greek yogurt

salt and black pepper

1. Use a small, sharp knife to peel and segment the lemon. Roughly chop the segments into 3–4 pieces and put them into a large bowl, then squeeze what's left of the membrane into the bowl (you want about 1½ teaspoons of juice).

2. Add the fava beans, lettuce, herbs, 2 tablespoons of olive oil, ¼ teaspoon of salt, and a good grind of pepper to the bowl of lemon and toss everything together well.

3. Mix together the toum and yogurt, and spread out on a large platter. Top with the salad, slightly to one side. Drizzle all over with the remaining 1 tablespoon of olive oil and serve.

Make it your own:
  – Veganize it: use a dairy-free alternative for the yogurt.
  – Use defrosted peas in place of the fava beans, and any mixture of herbs and leaves you have on hand.

(That one bag of) mixed veggies and potato fritters with harissa

Prep time: *25 minutes*
Cook time: *1 hour 20 minutes*
Chilling time: *30 minutes*

This fritter is inspired by Moroccan maakouda—a street-side snack of fried potato cakes, usually stuffed into a sandwich with plenty of harissa. This version utilizes that one bag of frozen mixed veggies sitting in the back of your freezer, and bypasses the sandwich route altogether (although you could, by all means, go in that direction!). Serve these hot or at room temperature; they won't be as crispy once they've been sitting for a bit, but they will still taste wonderful.

Makes 16 fritters

2 russet potatoes, *peeled and cut into 1¼-inch/3cm chunks (2½ cups/500g)*

9 oz/250g frozen mixed vegetables, *steamed according to package directions and drained*

2 garlic cloves, *roughly chopped*

½ cup/10g parsley, *roughly chopped*

2½ tsp cumin seeds, *toasted and roughly crushed with a mortar and pestle*

1 large egg

2 tsp finely grated lemon zest

¼ cup/30g all-purpose flour

3 cups/700ml vegetable oil, *for deep-frying*

salt and black pepper

BATTER

⅔ cup/85g all-purpose flour

⅓ cup/40g cornstarch

1¼ tsp fast-acting dry yeast

⅔ tsp baking powder

⅔ tsp ground turmeric

½ cup plus 2 tbsp/145ml lukewarm water

HARISSA DIP

1½ tbsp rose harissa, *or 2¼ tsp Tunisian harissa*

2 tbsp lemon juice

1½ tsp honey

2 garlic cloves, *minced*

2 tbsp olive oil

1. Put the potatoes and 2 teaspoons of salt into a medium saucepan, for which you have a lid, and add enough water to cover by about 1¼ inches/3cm. Bring to a boil on medium-high heat, then lower the heat to medium, cover, and cook for 8 minutes, or until easily pierced with a knife. Drain well, then, when cool enough to handle, use a potato ricer to rice the potatoes into a large bowl.

2. While the potatoes are cooking, put the steamed mixed vegetables, garlic, and parsley into a food processor and pulse a few times until everything is finely chopped. Add to the bowl of potatoes along with the cumin, egg, lemon zest, 1 teaspoon of salt, and a good grind of pepper. Mix to combine, then refrigerate for 30 minutes, to firm up slightly.

3. Make the dip by whisking together all the ingredients in a small bowl with a tiny pinch of salt.

4. Make the batter by whisking together all the ingredients with ⅓ teaspoon of salt in a medium bowl. Set aside to bubble up for about 20 minutes.

5. Meanwhile, put the ¼ cup/30g of flour into a shallow bowl. Use your hands to form 1½ oz/40–45g patties (about 2 inches/5cm in diameter) of the potato mixture and dip each one into the flour to coat, shaking off the excess. You should make about 16 patties— don't worry if they're not perfect.

6. Heat the vegetable oil in a medium, high-sided sauté pan over medium-high heat. Test it is hot by dropping a bit of batter into the oil—it should sizzle almost immediately. Working one at a time, dip each potato patty into the batter to coat, then drop it into the hot oil (don't worry if there are scraggly bits of batter— this adds to the look). Fry 6–7 at a time, for about 6–7 minutes, or until deeply golden. Use a slotted spoon to transfer them to a baking sheet lined with paper towels, sprinkle with a little salt, and continue with the rest.

7. Transfer the fritters to a serving plate and serve the harissa dip in a bowl alongside.

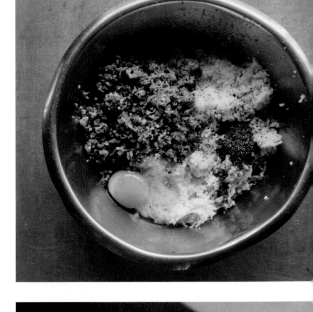

Make it your own:

- Serve with yogurt instead of the harissa dip to make this kid-friendly.
- Use up other frozen vegetables, such as peas or broccoli.
- Leave out the yeast if you can't get any.

_____

_____

_____

Creamed corn stuffed peppers with pickled jalapeños

Prep time: *20 minutes*
Cook time: *1 hour 15 minutes*

These impressive-looking peppers are deceptively easy to put together, and a sure way to put that bag of frozen corn to good use. Eat this alongside the fava bean and herb salad (p. 195) or some roasted potatoes, for a complete meal.

Serves 4, as a light lunch

1 green jalapeño, *thinly sliced, seeds and all* (1½ tbsp)
2 tbsp apple cider vinegar
1 tsp sugar
1½ cups/250g frozen corn kernels, *defrosted*
7 tbsp/100ml heavy cream
⅓ cup/50g instant polenta
3 garlic cloves, *minced*
1 large egg
7 tbsp/105ml olive oil
⅔ cup/75g coarsely grated low-moisture mozzarella
⅔ cup/75g coarsely grated mature cheddar
4 medium red romano peppers
2 onions, *cut into 5 x ½-inch/ 1cm-thick rounds*
¼ oz/5g thyme sprigs
½ cup/10g cilantro, *finely chopped*
salt and black pepper

Get ahead:
– Prepare and stuff the peppers a day ahead, ready to be baked on the day.

1. Preheat the oven to 400°F.

2. Put the jalapeño, vinegar, and sugar into a small bowl and mix to combine. Set aside to pickle.

3. Put the corn, cream, polenta, two-thirds of the garlic, the egg, 1 tablespoon of oil, ¾ teaspoon of salt, and a generous grind of pepper into a food processor and pulse to a very rough purée. Transfer to a bowl and stir in the cheeses.

4. Use a small, sharp knife to make an incision lengthwise into each pepper (making sure not to cut through the ends), keeping the stem intact. Gently use your fingers to remove and discard the seeds, then stuff each pepper with the corn mixture.

5. Put 1 tablespoon of oil in the base of a large, cast-iron saucepan or sauté pan and then top with the onion rounds and thyme to cover the base, sprinkling with a little salt and pepper. Place the peppers, slit side up, on top of the onions and drizzle them with 1 tablespoon of oil. Season lightly with salt and pepper, then pour ¾ cup plus 2 tablespoons/200ml of water into the pan, making sure not to pour it on top of the peppers. Bake for 30 minutes, then turn the heat up to 425°F and bake for another 20 minutes, or until everything is soft and nicely colored.

6. Meanwhile, put the remaining 4 tablespoons of oil, the cilantro, the remaining garlic, ⅛ teaspoon of salt, and a good grind of pepper into a small bowl and stir to combine.

7. Spoon the cilantro oil and pickled jalapeños over the peppers and serve warm.

Make it your own:
– Use regular red bell peppers cut in half lengthwise if you can't find romano.
– Play with the cheeses— anything oozy and melty will work here!
– Double this recipe if cooking for a larger crowd.

_____
_____
_____
_____

Greens and chermoula potato pie

Prep time: *30 minutes*
Cook time: *1 hour
25 minutes*
Chilling time: *20 minutes +*

We're constantly feeding off each other's vibes at the OTK; someone will make a dish, setting off a series of inspirational takes out of which a number of new dishes are born. Verena came up with this pie, saying, "I love how you savory chefs use greens and herbs so liberally." V obviously went one step further, making her own pastry like the true pastry chef that she is. We use store-bought puff here, but you can always take a page out of V's book and make the pastry, if you like.

Serves 4, generously

4 tbsp/60ml olive oil

2 onions, *thinly sliced
(12¾ oz/360g)*

12¼ oz/350g frozen
spinach, *defrosted and
drained of excess water*

¾ cup/15g dill, *roughly
chopped*

1½ tsp finely grated lemon
zest

1 frozen all-butter puff
pastry sheet, *defrosted
(11½ oz/325g)*

4½ oz/130g Greek
feta, *roughly crumbled*

1 russet potato, *skin on and
scrubbed clean, then sliced
paper thin (9 oz/250g)*

CHERMOULA

5 garlic cloves, *roughly
chopped*

1 small Fresno chile, *roughly
chopped, seeds and all
(1 tbsp)*

2 tsp cumin seeds, *toasted
and roughly crushed with
a mortar and pestle*

1 tsp paprika

1½ cups/30g cilantro,
roughly chopped

4 tbsp/60ml olive oil

1½ tbsp lemon juice

salt and black pepper

1. For the chermoula, put the garlic, chile, cumin, paprika, cilantro, ½ teaspoon of salt, a good grind of pepper, and 3 tablespoons of oil into a food processor and pulse into a coarse paste. Set aside.

2. Next, make the pie filling. Put 3 tablespoons of oil into a large sauté pan on medium-high heat. Once the oil is hot, add the onions and cook, stirring occasionally, for about 12 minutes, or until softened and well browned. Add half the chermoula paste, the spinach, 1 teaspoon of salt, and a good grind of pepper, and cook for 2–3 minutes more. Remove from the heat and add the dill and lemon zest. Set aside to cool, about 20 minutes.

3. Line a 9½-inch/24cm tart pan with a piece of parchment paper large enough to cover the bottom and a little bit over the sides (the excess will help you lift out the tart when it's baked). Lay the puff pastry on top, cutting away any excess overhang and using the extra pastry to fill any gaps. You want the pastry to evenly fit the bottom and sides of the pan.

4. Poke the bottom all over (about 10 times) with a fork, then spread the cooled spinach mixture over it evenly. Sprinkle with the feta, then roughly crimp the pastry edges to create a ¾-inch/2cm rim around the pie. Refrigerate the pie for at least 20 minutes—you want to bake it from cold.

5. Preheat the oven to 400°F.

6. Toss the potato together in a bowl with 1 tablespoon of oil, ½ teaspoon of salt, and a good grind of pepper. Fan out the slices in a circular pattern, overlapping slightly, to cover the filling but not the pastry rim.

7. Bake the pie from cold for 45–50 minutes, or until cooked through and nicely colored. Set aside to cool, about 15 minutes.

8. When ready to serve, stir the lemon juice and the remaining 1 tablespoon of oil into the rest of the chermoula. Spoon half of this all over the pie, serving the remainder in a bowl alongside.

Make it your own:
- Swap out the frozen spinach for other greens such as kale or chard.
- Veganize it: leave out the feta and use vegan puff pastry for the crust.

_____

_____

_____

Get ahead:

– Assemble the pie (minus
  the potato) a day ahead
  and keep refrigerated.

Skillet berries, bread, and browned butter

Prep time: *15 minutes*
Cook time: *1 hour*

This is a great way to use up all the bits: a bag of frozen berries, those oats at the back of your pantry, that bread that really needs using up. The inspiration for this dish was the very British summer pudding, its simple combination of soft bread and berries winning the hearts of the nation. Like many of our dishes, it took a bit of a left-field turn and landed right here, in this cozy place of browned butter and oats, toasted sourdough, and sweet spiced fruit. Serve this as a brunch dish or a late afternoon treat.

Serves 6

4 large Braeburn apples *(1 lb 7 oz/650g), peeled, cored and each cut into 6 wedges*

1½ tsp ground star anise, *plus an extra ¼ tsp to serve*

1½ tsp vanilla bean paste, *or vanilla extract*

½ cup plus 2 tbsp/130g unsalted butter

6 tbsp/75g sugar

4¼ oz/120g stale crustless sourdough, *roughly torn into ½-inch/1cm pieces*

1 cup/100g rolled oats

½ tsp flaked sea salt

3½ cups/500g frozen mixed berries, *kept frozen*

½ cup plus 2 tbsp/150ml heavy cream, *very cold*

1. Preheat the oven to 400°F.

2. Put the apples, ½ teaspoon of star anise, half the vanilla, 2 tablespoons/30g of butter, and half the sugar into a large, oven-safe sauté pan. Transfer to the oven to bake for 20–25 minutes, stirring halfway through, or until the apples have softened but still retain their shape.

3. While the apples are baking, put the remaining ½ cup/100g of butter into a large frying pan on medium-high heat. Once melted, cook for 4–4½ minutes, swirling the pan often, or until nicely browned and nutty. Transfer the browned butter to a large bowl and return the pan to the heat. Add the sourdough and toast for 2 minutes, stirring often, then add to the browned-butter bowl.

Next, toast the oats in the same way for 2 minutes and add them to the bowl. Add the salt, the remaining 1 teaspoon of star anise, and the remaining sugar, and stir everything together well.

4. When the apples are ready, stir in the frozen berries and 2 tablespoons of water and top with the bread mixture. Turn the oven temperature down to 350°F and bake for 30 minutes, or until golden and bubbling. Let settle for 5–10 minutes, then sprinkle with the extra star anise.

5. Combine the cold cream and the remaining vanilla in a small bowl. Serve the crumble warm, with the cold cream to drizzle on top.

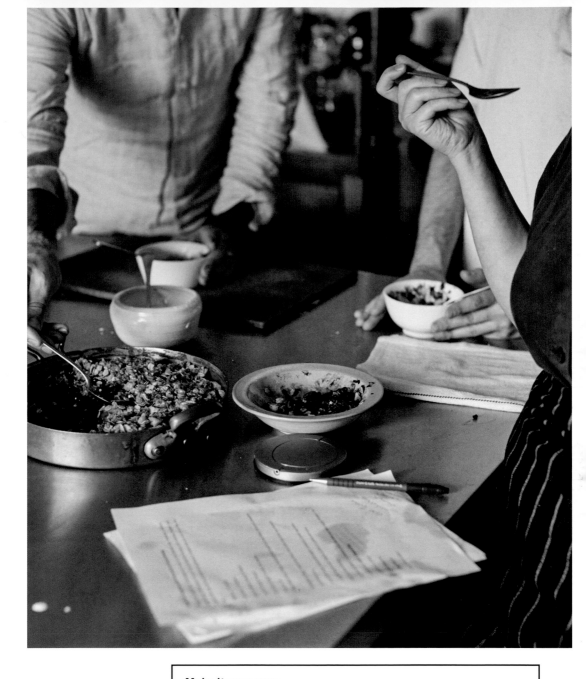

Make it your own:
- Use whatever mixture of frozen or fresh berries you have on hand.
- Play with the spices and bread, using up what you have in your pantry.
- Make this super decadent and swap out the cold cream for vanilla ice cream.

_____

_____

At
the
very

END.

At the very end

At the very end . . . or at the very beginning—we won't hold it against you either way—when you're craving something sweet to balance out the salty, we've got you covered. Ixta, Noor, and Chaya cook mostly savory things, but that's not to say they don't delve into the world of sweet treats from time to time. Verena, on the other hand, with baking very much a part of her DNA, lives and breathes this world, speaking with the detailed precision of a chef who understands that baking and pastry is, in fact, a science. To fully understand it—the whats, whys, and hows—you must first wrap your mind around the delicate chemistry behind it (cue the chocoflan, p. 226).

We often joke that Noor and Ixta approach pastry with a much more "wing it and see what happens" attitude. Verena watches them, amused, politely biting her tongue at the possible disasters that might ensue. There have been too many to count, really, the two savory chefs frequently frustrated at their ongoing sugar-laced catastrophes. Interestingly enough, their headstrong approach often works, exploring flavor combinations and methods that might be slightly radical (see cheesy fruity stromboli, funky faloodeh, or sticky miso bananas on p. 232, 215, and 240 respectively). The point being that, at the Test Kitchen, baking is one part science and two parts sheer determination.

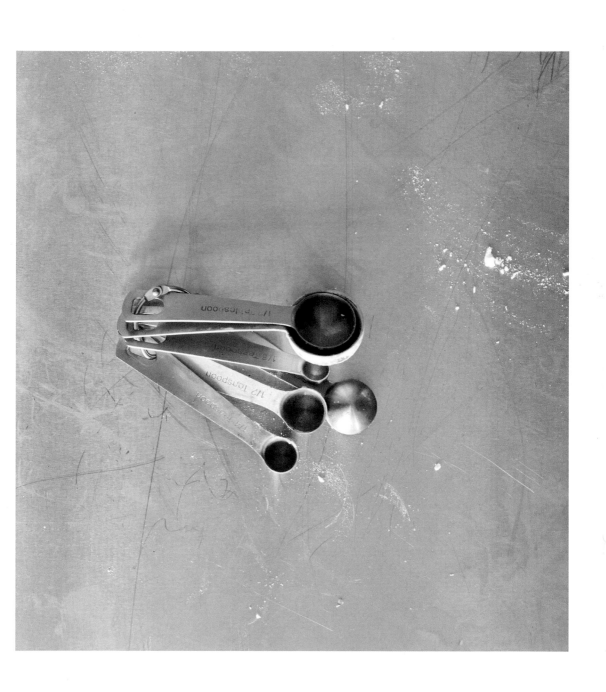

Carrot cake sandwich cookies

Prep time: *20 minutes*
Cook time: *1 hour*

These cookies are more cake than cookie, like a carrot cake in bite size. Not dissimilar to an American whoopie pie, you could say.

There's a significant amount of science involved in cookie making, despite what the Cookie Monster will have you believe. They can be temperamental at the best of times, really, so do make sure you follow these steps to ensure happy sandwich cookies and happy bellies all around. Don't over-whip the butter and cream cheese, for example, make sure they're softened at room temperature, and make sure that the cookies are nicely spread out on your sheet before baking too.

Makes 15 sandwich cookies

CARROT CAKE

2 cups/250g all-purpose flour

1¼ tsp baking soda

1 tsp baking powder

1½ tsp ground cinnamon

1 tsp ground ginger

¼ tsp ground cloves

½ tsp salt

1 cup/100g pecans, *toasted and finely chopped*

⅓ cup/30g dried shredded coconut

2¾ cups/300g finely grated carrots *(from about 3 or 4 carrots)*

½ cup/115g unsalted butter, *softened at room temperature*

packed ½ cup/100g light brown sugar

½ cup/100g granulated sugar

2 large eggs

2 tsp vanilla bean paste

mounded ½ cup/80g golden raisins

CREAM CHEESE FILLING

6 tbsp/90g unsalted butter, *at room temperature*

1 cup/125g confectioners' sugar, *sifted, plus 2 tsp extra for dusting*

8 oz/225g full-fat cream cheese, *at room temperature*

2½ tsp finely grated orange zest

1. Preheat the oven to 400°F. Line two large baking sheets with parchment paper.

2. In a large bowl, whisk together the flour, baking soda, baking powder, spices, salt, pecans, and coconut. Set aside.

3. Use your hands to squeeze out as much liquid as possible from the carrots—you want 7 oz/200g of grated carrot after it has been wrung out.

4. Put the butter and both sugars into the bowl of a stand mixer, with the paddle attachment in place, and beat on medium speed for 90 seconds, until just combined. Add the eggs, one at a time, then, once incorporated, add the vanilla, carrots, and golden raisins and mix to combine. Turn the speed to low and gradually add the dry ingredients, mixing until just incorporated. Clean the mixer bowl and paddle attachment to use later.

5. Transfer the mixture to a piping bag and snip the end to make an opening about 1 inch/2½cm wide. Pipe heaped tablespoons of the mixture, about 1¼ oz/35g in weight and 2–2½ inches/5–6cm in diameter, onto your prepared baking sheets, using your fingers to round them off slightly (don't flatten them). Bake for 10 minutes, or until just cooked through but soft to the touch. Let cool slightly before gently transferring them to a wire rack to cool completely. Repeat to make 30 cookies in total.

Get ahead:

– Make the cookies and filling separately up to 2 days ahead. Store the cookies in an airtight container and keep the filling refrigerated. Assemble when ready to serve.

Make it your own:

- Play around with the spices, nuts, and dried fruit, keeping the same weights.

_____

_____

_____

_____

6. Meanwhile, make the filling. Beat the butter and confectioners' sugar together in the bowl of the stand mixer, with the paddle attachment in place, on medium speed for 5 minutes, until very light and fluffy. Measure out the cream cheese in a separate small bowl and mix briefly with a spatula until smooth. Add to the creamed butter and confectioners' sugar, along with the orange zest, and beat until just combined. Chill for 10 minutes to firm up a little before using.

7. Once the cookies have cooled, pair them up—trying to match similar sizes. Spoon a generous 1 tablespoon of the cream cheese filling onto the flat side of one cookie. Top with the flat side of the other cookie to make a sandwich. Repeat to make 15 sandwiches in total. Dust the tops of the cookies with the extra confectioners' sugar and serve on the same day.

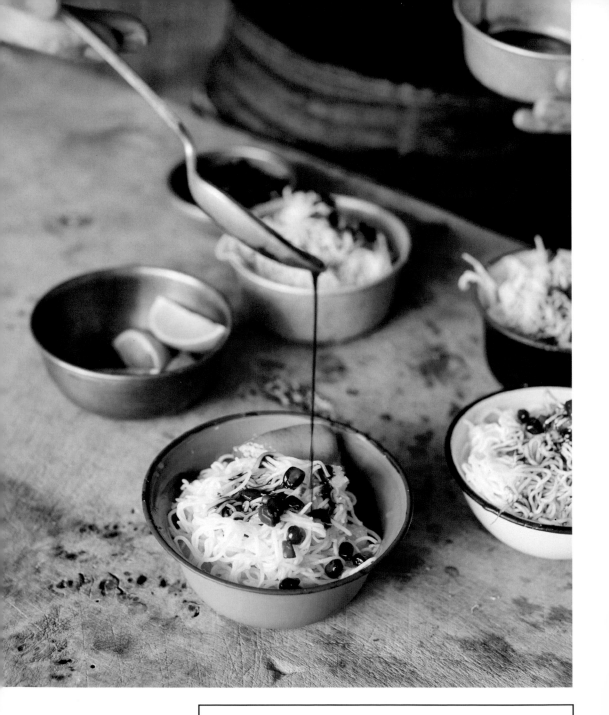

Make it your own:
– Use lemon juice instead of the lime, and raspberry or strawberry purée in place of the pomegranate syrup.

Funky faloodeh

Prep time: *15 minutes*
Cook time: *1 hour*
Freezing time: *6 hours to overnight*

Faloodeh is a popular Persian dessert made up of cold vermicelli noodles mixed with frozen granita or ice cream, and comes in many different forms and flavors. It might seem a little strange to those unaccustomed to noodles for dessert, but trust us: it is cold, sweet, and refreshing and just what's needed on a hot summer day. It's also super quirky and fun to make (and to look at)! Make sure that all your components are set and, once you're ready, put them together quickly and only just before serving.

Serves 6

1 cup plus 2 tbsp/220g
  sugar
1 cup/20g mint sprigs
½ cup plus 2 tbsp/150ml
  lime juice
3½ oz/100g dried vermicelli
  rice noodles *(we use Thai Taste)*

POMEGRANATE SYRUP
¾ cup plus 2 tbsp/200ml
  pomegranate juice
  (unsweetened)
1 tbsp sugar
1½ tsp good-quality rose
  water

TO SERVE
3 tbsp pomegranate seeds
1 large lime: *finely grate the zest to get 1½ tsp and then cut into 6 wedges*

Get ahead:
– Make the syrup, cooked noodles, and frozen granita the day before.

---

1. Put the sugar, 1¼ cups/300ml of water, and the mint into a medium saucepan on medium-high heat. Bring to a simmer, stirring to dissolve the sugar, then add the lime juice and set aside to cool completely.

2. Strain the mixture through a sieve into a freezer-proof container, discarding the solids, then cover and freeze for about 2 hours. Use a fork to scrape at the half-frozen mixture, then return to the freezer and continue in this way, scraping at the mixture every half hour or so, for a total of 4 hours.

3. Cook the noodles in plenty of boiling water for 6 minutes, or until very soft (you want to overcook them slightly). Drain well, then use a pair of kitchen scissors to cut the noodles roughly in half.

4. Make the pomegranate syrup by putting the juice and sugar into a medium saucepan and placing it on medium heat. Cook for 20–25 minutes, until reduced to the consistency of maple

syrup. Stir in the rose water and set aside to cool.

5. When you are nearly ready to serve the faloodeh, fill a large bowl with cold water and plenty of ice and add the cooked vermicelli noodles. Refrigerate for about 15 minutes.

6. Remove the lime granita from the fridge 5–10 minutes before you want to serve it, scraping at it with a fork to get that snowflake effect.

7. Working quickly, drain the noodles well in a sieve, wipe out the bowl, then return the noodles to the bowl along with half the granita and toss to combine. Some of the noodles will start to solidify a little (that's what you want). Divide the mixture among six small bowls or martini glasses, and top with the remaining granita. Add a spoonful of the pomegranate syrup to each bowl, then sprinkle with the pomegranate seeds and lime zest. Serve each bowl with a lime wedge to squeeze on top.

Coconut dream cake

Prep time: *15 minutes*
Cook time: *1 hour 20 minutes to 1 hour 50 minutes*

Get ahead:
- Make the topping up to 3 days ahead and keep in an airtight container.
- Bake the cakes a day ahead; wrap well.

Yotam and Noor had differing opinions when it came to this cake. Yotam, team one-layer, and Noor, team two-layers, because why have one when you can have two? Verena soon came into the conversation and swiftly voted for team two-layers (much to Noor's delight), but although there was a clear winner, we've decided to let you take charge—the cake can be baked in two 8-inch/20cm round cake pans, creating that "sandwich" effect, or one large rectangular one. Either way, this cake is an absolute dream (because surely dreams are laced with coconut, cardamom, and sugar). Double or triple up on the coconut topping here—it's ridiculously delicious snacking material.

Serves 8

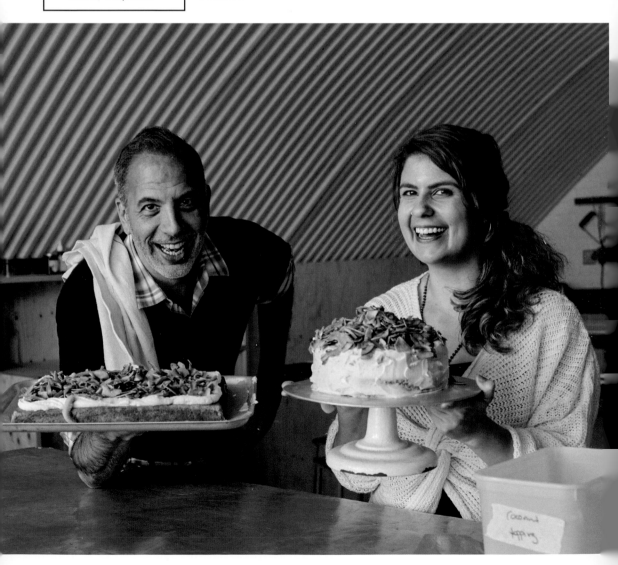

- 2½ cups/320g all-purpose flour
- 15 cardamom pods, *shells discarded and seeds roughly crushed with a mortar and pestle*
- ½ tsp baking soda
- 3¾ tsp baking powder
- ½ tsp salt
- 1½ cups/300g granulated sugar
- ¾ cup/170g unsalted butter, *softened at room temperature, then roughly cut into 1¼-inch/3cm cubes, plus extra for greasing*
- 5 large egg whites, *at room temperature*
- 7 tbsp/120g Greek yogurt, *at room temperature*
- 1 tbsp vanilla bean paste, *or the seeds scraped from 1 vanilla pod*
- 1 cup/240ml full-fat coconut milk

COCONUT FROSTING
- ¾ cup plus 2 tbsp/200g unsalted butter, *softened at room temperature, then roughly cut into 1¼-inch/3cm cubes*
- 1¼ cups/150g confectioners' sugar, *sifted*
- 5¼ oz/150g full-fat cream cheese, *at room temperature*

COCONUT TOPPING
- mounded 1 cup/100g dried coconut flakes (*aka coconut chips*)
- 3 tbsp maple syrup
- 10 cardamom pods, *shells discarded and seeds roughly crushed with a mortar and pestle*
- ¼ tsp salt

1. Preheat the oven to 350°F. Grease and use parchment paper to line the bottom and sides of two 8-inch/20cm round cake pans or one rectangular baking pan, 9 x 13 inches/23 x 33cm and 1½ inches/4cm deep.

2. Put the flour, cardamom, baking soda, baking powder, and salt into a large bowl and whisk together to combine.

3. Put the granulated sugar and butter into the bowl of a stand mixer, with the paddle attachment in place, and beat on medium-high speed until light and fluffy, about 4 minutes. Scrape down the sides of the bowl, turn the speed to medium, and add the egg whites, mixing to just incorporate, then add the yogurt and vanilla bean paste and beat for 30 seconds. Scrape down the sides of the bowl and turn the speed down to low. Add a third of the flour mixture and a third of the coconut milk, alternating until both are combined and the mixture is smooth.

4. Team two-layers: Transfer half the mixture, about 1 lb 6 oz/630g, to each prepared pan and bake for 35 minutes, or until a skewer inserted into the center comes out clean. Set aside to cool slightly before very carefully releasing them from their pans and inverting them onto a cake stand or plate. Let cool completely.

5. Team one-layer: Transfer the mixture to the prepared rectangular baking pan and bake for 35 minutes, or until a skewer inserted into the center comes out clean. Set aside to cool completely.

6. Meanwhile, make the topping by putting the coconut flakes, maple syrup, cardamom, and salt on a parchment-lined baking sheet and tossing to combine. Bake for 8 minutes, give everything a good stir, then bake for 5 minutes more, or until nicely browned and crispy. Set aside to cool and crisp up further.

7. Once the cakes have cooled, make the frosting. Add the butter and sugar to the stand mixer, with the paddle attachment in place, and beat on medium-high speed until light and creamy, about 5 minutes. Beat the cream cheese in a bowl until smooth, then add to the stand mixer with the creamed butter and mix on medium-low until just combined and no longer streaky.

8. Team two-layers: Spread a little less than half the frosting on one of the inverted cakes, spreading to cover the top. Gently invert the second cake on top, so that the bottom is now the top. Spread the remaining frosting around the top and sides of the cake, using an offset spatula to help you. Don't worry if it looks a little messy; this is all part of its charm. Lastly top with the coconut topping so that it covers the top of the cake, leaving the sides exposed.

9. Team one-layer: Spread the frosting all over the top of the cake, creating little grooves and waves with your spatula. Top with the coconut topping.

10. Refrigerate if not serving right away, adding the coconut topping just before serving.

Upside-down lemon, maple, and vanilla cake with lemon-maple butter

Prep time: *15 minutes*
Cook time: *1 hour 40 minutes*

This magnificent cake was made with the purpose of showcasing winter lemons, their bitter flesh a great way to cut through an otherwise decadent eating experience. As happy accidents go, this was tested alongside a separate dish that included a maple-butter sauce. A squeeze of lemon and a generous amount of maple butter was spooned over the cake because well, why not, and it suddenly dawned on us that lemon-maple butter had been the missing component all along. Lesson learned: sometimes that which is very, very wrong can turn out to be really quite right.

Be sure to remove the butter for the cake from the fridge well in advance—it needs to be super softened at room temperature before making the base.

Serves 8

3 medium lemons, *thinly sliced into ¹⁄₁₆-inch/¼cm-thick rounds to get 24 slices, seeds removed*

⅔ cup/160ml maple syrup

1 vanilla pod, *halved lengthwise, seeds scraped and reserved with the pod*

1¾ cups plus 1 tbsp/225g all-purpose flour

2 tsp baking powder

¼ tsp salt

1 cup/225g unsalted butter, *softened at room temperature, then cut into ¾-inch/2cm cubes*

3 large eggs, *plus 1 large egg yolk*

packed 1 cup plus 1 tbsp/ 225g light brown sugar

¼ cup/60ml whole milk

1 cup/240g crème fraîche, *to serve*

1. Preheat the oven to 375°F. Line a baking dish about 9 x 13 inches/23 x 33cm in size with a piece of parchment paper large enough to cover the bottom and sides, with enough overhang to fold over the cake as well.

2. Place a large, nonstick frying pan on high heat and, once very hot, char a third of the lemon slices on both sides—about 1–2 minutes per side. Continue in this way with the rest.

3. Put ½ cup/120ml of maple syrup and the scraped-out vanilla pod in the bottom of the prepared baking dish. Top with the charred lemon slices, spreading out so they cover the entire bottom, overlapping in places.

4. Sift the flour, baking powder, and salt into the bowl of a stand mixer, with the whisk attachment in place, and mix on medium speed to combine. Add the softened butter, eggs, yolk, vanilla seeds, brown sugar, milk, and the remaining 3 tablespoons of maple syrup, and mix on medium speed for 2 minutes until combined. The mixture will look as if it's split a little with some smaller cubes of butter—but that's okay.

5. Spoon the mixture into a piping bag, snipping the base, and pipe the mixture evenly on top of the lemons in the baking dish (piping the mixture ensures the lemons don't move around too much). Gently smooth over the mixture with the back of a spoon. Fold over the excess parchment paper to cover, then wrap the dish tightly in foil.

LEMON-MAPLE BUTTER

3 tbsp lemon juice

½ cup/120ml maple syrup

½ cup/115g unsalted butter, *fridge cold and cut into ½-inch/1½cm cubes*

6. Place the baking dish in a larger roasting pan (roughly 16 x 11 inches/40 x 28cm). Pour enough boiling water into the pan to come 1¼ inches/3cm up the sides (about 1 quart/1 liter), then bake for 70 minutes, or until a toothpick inserted into the center comes out clean. Remove the foil, unwrap the top of the cake, and lift out the baking dish from the water. Set aside for 5 minutes before carefully inverting the whole thing onto a platter, removing the parchment paper to expose the lemons.

7. Toward the last 10 minutes of cooking, make the lemon-maple butter. Put the lemon juice and maple syrup into a small saucepan and bring to a simmer on medium-high heat. Cook for about 2 minutes, then turn the heat down to low and, when no longer simmering, gradually add the butter cubes a little at a time, whisking with each addition until incorporated. Don't let the mixture boil at all—you should be left with an emulsified sauce. Remove from the heat.

8. Drizzle one-third of the lemon-maple butter all over the cake and serve warm, with the extra maple butter and crème fraîche alongside.

Make it your own:

– Try this recipe using kumquats instead of lemons and orange juice instead of lemon juice.

_____

_____

_____

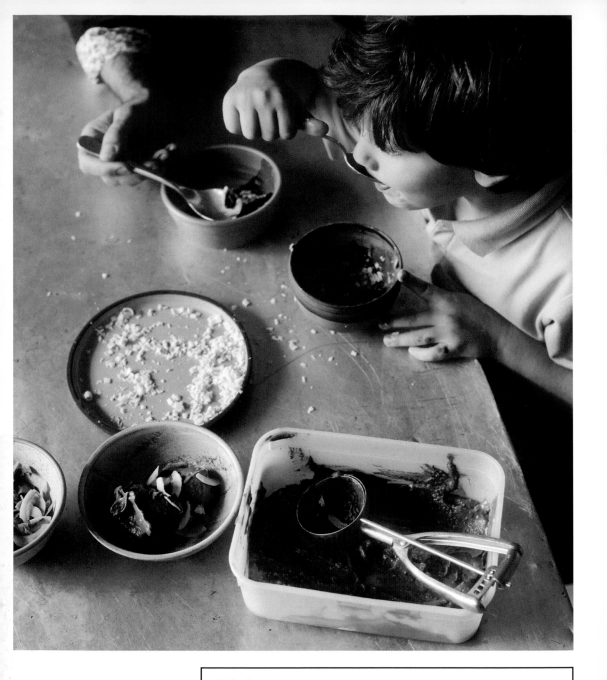

Make it your own:

- Use any frozen berries you like, or mix it up by adding some frozen mango or banana.
- Go crazy with your choice of toppings: nuts, fruits, and any type of chocolate shavings!

_____

_____

_____

Frozen berries for little humans

Prep time: *10 minutes*
Cook time: *5 minutes*
Freezing time: *30–40 minutes*

Bags of frozen berries are a sure way to quick-fix a sweet craving. This recipe is courtesy of our colleague Claudine Boulstridge, who is always on the lookout for creative ways to feed her three kids, and to keep the options healthy . . . ish. A great one for the little humans, but the adults sort of (really!) like it too.

Serves 4 little humans

1½ cups/350g frozen raspberries, *kept frozen*

½ cup plus 2 tbsp/140ml heavy cream, *fridge cold*

1 tbsp vanilla bean paste, *or the scraped seeds of 1 vanilla pod*

3 tbsp confectioners' sugar

2 tbsp pomegranate molasses

TOPPING

1½ oz/40g white chocolate, *peeled with a vegetable peeler to make curls*

⅓ cup/30g dried coconut flakes, *well toasted*

1. Put all the ingredients, except the chocolate and coconut flakes, into a food processor and blitz until completely smooth, scraping down the sides of the bowl as needed. Transfer to a freezer-proof container, for which you have a lid, cover, and freeze for just 30–40 minutes (you want it to be a loose, soft-serve consistency).

2. Scoop into four small bowls and sprinkle with the white chocolate and coconut flakes.

Verena's road trip cookies

Prep time: *10 minutes*
Cook time: *1 hour 15 minutes*
Chilling time: *2 hours to overnight*

A few members of the OTK gang took a road trip to Durdle Door—"a nice road trip out of London," said Verena, but it was more to satisfy Noor's constant quest for sunshine. Gitai soon took charge of the music, and off to the beach they went. Halfway through the journey, the mid-morning munchies kicked in and Verena whipped out a box of her homemade oatmeal cookies, baked fresh that morning. They smelled of cinnamon and hugs, were the perfect ratio of chewy to soft, and, beyond anything, it was V's cookies that made the trip so wonderfully sweet.

Makes 28 cookies

1¼ cups/275g unsalted butter, *cut into ¾-inch/2cm cubes, at room temperature*

packed ¾ cup plus 1 tbsp/175g light brown sugar

6 tbsp/75g granulated sugar

4 tsp/20g vanilla bean paste, *or vanilla extract*

2 cups/180g rolled oats

1⅔ cups/155g oat bran

¾ cup/100g all-purpose flour

1 tsp ground cinnamon

¾ tsp freshly grated nutmeg

¼ tsp baking powder

1 tsp baking soda

1 tsp salt

1⅓ cups/200g raisins or golden raisins *(or a mix)*

1 large egg

1. Put 5 tablespoons/75g of the butter, both sugars, and the vanilla into a large bowl, mix to combine, and set aside.

2. Put the rolled oats, oat bran, flour, cinnamon, nutmeg, baking powder, baking soda, salt, and raisins (or golden raisins) into a separate large bowl and mix together to combine.

3. Put the remaining ¾ cup plus 2 tablespoons/200g of butter into a medium saucepan on medium heat and allow to melt and bubble away, whisking every now and then. As the butter browns, it will begin to foam, color, and smell nutty—keep whisking and, once it turns deeply brown, remove from the heat, about 6–7 minutes in total. Immediately pour the browned butter into the bowl containing the cubed butter and sugars and whisk until combined (it will look separated with the butter sitting on top, but that's okay).

4. Set aside for 10 minutes to cool slightly, stirring once or twice. Add the egg and whisk until combined. Next add the contents of the oats bowl and use a rubber spatula to mix into a soft dough. Cover the surface of the dough and transfer to the fridge to rest and firm up for 2 hours, or overnight. If the latter, remove from the fridge about 1 hour before baking.

5. Preheat the oven to 375°F. Roll the dough into 28 balls, each roughly 1½ oz/40g in weight, and transfer 6–8 balls, well spaced apart, to a large, parchment-lined baking sheet.

6. Bake each batch of cookies for 4 minutes, then rotate the sheet and bake for 4–5 minutes more. The cookies will have set and lightly browned around the edges and will look puffy and under-baked in the middle. Let each batch cool for about 15 minutes before eating them warm, or devouring them later at room temperature.

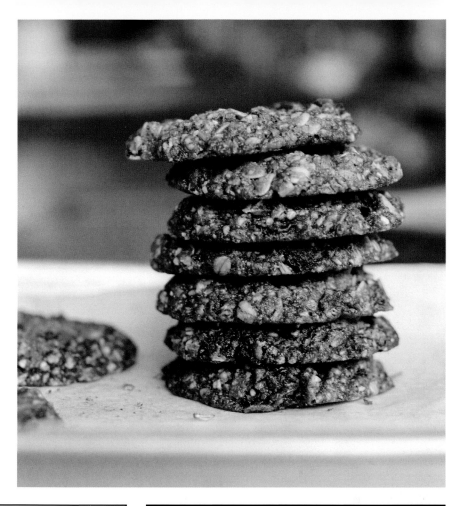

Get ahead:

- Store any extra baked cookies in an airtight container—they will keep for up to 2 days (if they last that long).
- Keep any unbaked cookie dough in the fridge for up to 3 days, baking as you need.

Chocoflan

Prep time: *10 minutes*
Cook time: *1 hour 20 minutes*
Cooling time: *3 hours to overnight*

"So bad, it's good" couldn't be more fitting than for chocoflan, a dessert that combines two layers of pure decadence into one cake (think brownie meets flan). There's also a nifty science trick involved, where the cake layer and flan layer swap positions during the baking, adding to the kitchen wizardry. We've tested this using different pans, without much success, so do make sure you use a 10½-inch/27cm bundt pan that does not have a removable base.

Serves 10–12

½ cup/160g caramel sauce
  (thick set), store-bought
  or homemade (we used
  Waitrose salted caramel
  dipping sauce)

1 tbsp whole milk

CHOCOLATE CAKE

2 cups/250g all-purpose
  flour

½ tsp baking powder

½ tsp baking soda

¾ cup/70g cocoa powder

¼ tsp salt

½ cup/115g unsalted
  butter, *softened at room
  temperature, plus extra for
  greasing*

½ cup/100g dark
  muscovado sugar

½ cup plus 2 tbsp/125g
  granulated sugar

2 large eggs

¾ cup plus 2 tbsp/200ml
  buttermilk *(8 oz/220g)*

FLAN

1 (12 oz/354ml) can of
  evaporated milk

1 (14 oz/397g) can of
  sweetened condensed
  milk

4¼ oz/120g full-fat
  cream cheese, *at room
  temperature*

3 large eggs

2 tsp vanilla bean paste,
  or vanilla extract

¼ tsp salt

1. Preheat the oven to 375°F. Liberally grease a 10½-inch/27cm bundt pan with butter, then coat the bottom with half the caramel sauce. Place the bundt pan in a larger roasting pan about 16 x 11 inches/40 x 28cm in size and set aside.

2. For the cake batter, sift the flour, baking powder, baking soda, cocoa powder, and salt into a medium bowl. Put the butter and both sugars into the bowl of a stand mixer with the paddle attachment in place. Beat on medium speed until light and fluffy, about 2 minutes. Add the eggs one at a time and beat until just incorporated, then turn the speed to medium-low. Add a third of the flour mixture and half the buttermilk and continue in this way, ending with the flour. Mix until everything is just incorporated, then transfer to the bundt pan, smoothing the batter evenly with the back of a spoon.

3. For the flan batter, put all the ingredients into a blender and blitz until smooth. Pour the flan batter over the cake batter, then cover the bundt pan with a circular piece of parchment paper, followed by a piece of foil, and wrap tightly. Add enough boiling water to the roasting pan to come about ¾ inch/2cm up the sides of the bundt pan. Transfer to the oven and bake for 80 to 90 minutes, rotating halfway through, or until a skewer inserted into the cake comes out almost clean. Remove from the water bath, removing the foil and parchment, and let cool for 1 hour (it won't be completely cool).

4. Invert the chocoflan onto a large round serving platter, shaking it slightly to release it from the pan, and refrigerate until completely cool, at least 2 hours or (preferably) overnight.

5. When ready to serve, thin out the remaining ¼ cup/80g of caramel with the 1 tablespoon of milk and drizzle all over the flan.

Get ahead:

– We really recommend
  making this the day before.
  It tastes best when it's fridge
  cold, and the flavors develop
  as it sits.

Muhallabieh with burnt honey orange syrup, kataifi, and pistachio sugar

Prep time: *10 minutes*
Cook time: *45 minutes*
Setting time: *3 hours to overnight*

Like two siblings, Gitai and Noor often bicker, and in this case, over the name of this dessert—Gitai insists on calling it "malabi," to which Noor rolls her eyes and says "muhallabieh." Either way, it's one and the same—the Middle Eastern equivalent of panna cotta, using rice or cornstarch to set the creamy base. This version uses a bitter orange syrup and crispy kataifi to give it the texture and tang it needs. You can find kataifi in any Middle Eastern grocery store, but roughly broken filo pastry would work here too.

Serves 6

2 cups plus 2 tbsp/500ml
  whole milk
¾ cup plus 2 tbsp/200ml
  heavy cream
¼ cup/50g sugar
¼ tsp flaked salt
½ cup/50g cornstarch
1 tsp good-quality orange
  blossom water

KATAIFI

2¼ oz/60g kataifi, *defrosted
  if frozen*
1½ tbsp unsalted butter,
  melted
1 tbsp olive oil
¼ cup/30g pistachios, *very
  lightly toasted*
1 tbsp sugar
¼ tsp flaked salt

*BURNT HONEY ORANGE
  SYRUP*

⅓ cup/120g honey
2 oranges: *1 squeezed to get
  ¼ cup/60ml juice and the
  other peeled and segmented*

1. Make sure to have six small glass bowls or glasses at the ready. Put the milk, cream, sugar, and salt into a medium saucepan and bring to a gentle simmer on medium heat.

2. In a medium bowl whisk together the cornstarch and ½ cup plus 1 tablespoon/130ml of water until smooth. Once the milk mixture has come to a simmer, slowly add the cornstarch mixture, whisking until smooth and similar in consistency to a thick custard, about 2 minutes. Stir in the orange blossom water and quickly divide the mixture among the glasses or bowls. Cover the tops with a piece of parchment paper or plastic wrap to prevent any skin from forming. Let cool down slightly, then transfer to the fridge to set, at least 3 hours, or overnight if you're getting ahead.

3. Preheat the oven to 400°F. Put the kataifi, butter, and oil into a bowl and toss to coat the strands. Using your fingers, gather about ⅓ oz/10g of the strands and tightly wrap them around your index finger, to create a sort of messy bundle. Transfer to a small,

parchment-lined baking sheet and continue to make bundles, six in total. Bake for 12–15 minutes, until deeply golden and cooked through.

4. Put the pistachios, sugar, and salt into the bowl of a food processor and pulse until very finely chopped. Once cool, toss the kataifi bundles with two-thirds of the pistachio sugar (don't worry if they break apart a little).

5. Meanwhile, make the syrup by putting the honey into a small saucepan on medium-high heat. Cook for 8–9 minutes, swirling the pan occasionally, until the honey turns a deep brown (don't be afraid to take it to the edge). Remove from the heat and add the orange juice. Set aside to cool. Roughly cut the orange segments into 3–4 pieces and add them to the syrup.

6. When ready to serve, remove the parchment paper (or plastic wrap) and top the muhallabieh with the syrup, a kataifi bundle, and a sprinkling of extra pistachio sugar. Serve cold.

Get ahead:
- Make the muhallabieh up to 2 days ahead, keeping them covered and refrigerated.
- Make the kataifi bundles up to 2 days ahead, keeping them in a well-sealed container.

Cheesy fruity stromboli

Prep time: *20 minutes*
Cook time: *1 hour 40 minutes*
Rising time: *1 hour*

Stromboli is basically a large piece of pizza dough that is rolled and stuffed with stuff. This fruity version straddles the line between sweet and savory, and is ideal for brunch or a late afternoon treat. This stromboli is best eaten fresh, on the day it is baked.

Serves 6

DOUGH

1½ cups/190g all-purpose flour

1½ tsp fast-acting dry yeast

1½ tsp granulated sugar

½ tsp salt

1½ tbsp olive oil, *plus extra for oiling*

7 tbsp/110ml lukewarm water

FILLING

3 small peaches
(12¼ oz/350g), pitted and each cut into 6 wedges (10½ oz/300g)

½ cup plus 2 tbsp/130g granulated sugar

1½ tbsp olive oil

1 cup/150g fresh blueberries

1½ tbsp cornstarch

½ cup/80g whole-milk ricotta

1 cup/120g coarsely grated low-moisture mozzarella

2 tsp lemon zest

½ tbsp thyme leaves, *plus some extra soft sprigs*

1 egg yolk

1 tbsp demerara sugar

1. Preheat the oven to 425°F.

2. Put all the dough ingredients into the bowl of a stand mixer with the dough hook in place. Beat on medium-high speed for 8 minutes, or until the dough is smooth (it will be a little sticky). Use oiled hands to transfer the dough to a lightly oiled, large bowl and cover with a damp kitchen towel. Set aside to double in size in a warm place, 1 hour.

3. Put the peaches, ½ cup/100g of granulated sugar, and the oil into a baking dish 9 x 13 inches/ 23 x 33cm in size. Mix everything and bake for 10 minutes. Add the blueberries and bake for 10 minutes more, or until the fruit has softened but still retains its shape. When cool, gently drain the mixture in a sieve set over a bowl, saving the liquid and the fruit. Put the fruit back into the baking dish and gently stir in 1 tablespoon of cornstarch.

4. Put the fruit liquid into a small sauté pan and place it on medium-high heat. Cook for 6–8 minutes, stirring occasionally, until reduced to a loose syrup. Set aside to cool and thicken.

5. Add the ricotta, mozzarella, lemon zest, the remaining ½ tablespoon cornstarch, and the remaining 2 tablespoons/30g granulated sugar to a bowl and mix well to combine.

6. Line a large baking sheet with parchment paper. Using well-oiled hands, transfer the dough to the lined sheet and gently stretch it out so it's about 8 x 11 inches/ 20 x 28cm in size.

7. Spread the ricotta mixture all over the dough, leaving a ¾-inch/ 2cm border around the edge.

8. Spoon the fruit mixture over the top, leaving a 1½-inch/4cm border around the edge. Sprinkle evenly with the thyme leaves.

9. With the longer end facing you, very gently pull the dough to roll the stromboli into a long cylinder shape, pushing the fruit filling inward and making it as compact as possible. Don't worry if you have a couple of small tears.

10. Arrange the thyme sprigs artfully on top, pushing them into the dough very gently, then brush with the egg yolk and sprinkle the top with the demerara sugar.

11. Bake for 10 minutes, then turn the heat down to 350°F and bake for 25 minutes more, until golden brown and cooked through. Remove from the oven and carefully transfer the stromboli to a wire rack. Let cool for about 20 minutes before serving, warm or at room temperature, with the fruit syrup alongside.

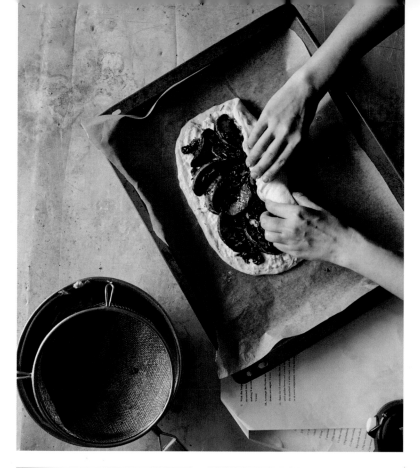

Get ahead:

– Make the dough the day
 ahead, leaving it to rise
 in the fridge overnight.
 Bring it back up to
 room temerature before
 working with it.

Almond, barberry, and orange brittle with Aleppo chile

Prep time: *25 minutes*
Cook time: *50 minutes*
Setting time: *1 hour 15 minutes*

This crunchy, sweet brittle is dangerously snackable and a great way to use up all the nuts and seeds hanging out in your cupboards. This is a good one to serve as an afternoon treat.

Serves 8, as a snack

2 tbsp heavy cream

½ cup/100g sugar

⅓ cup/80ml golden syrup *or light corn syrup*

5 tbsp/70g unsalted butter, *cut into roughly 1¼-inch/3cm cubes*

1 tsp vanilla bean paste, or *vanilla extract*

1 tsp flaked sea salt

1 tsp Aleppo chile, *or ½ tsp regular chile flakes*

1 tsp good-quality orange blossom water

½ oz/15g orange zest *(about 1½ tbsp finely grated zest, from 1–2 oranges)*

1¾ cups/150g sliced almonds, *lightly toasted*

¾ cup/90g pecan or walnut pieces, *lightly toasted then finely chopped*

¾ cup/90g pumpkin seeds, *lightly toasted*

¼ cup/40g sesame seeds, *lightly toasted*

¼ cup/20g barberries, *soaked in 7 tbsp/100ml boiling water for 10 minutes, then drained*

1 oz/30g dark chocolate, *roughly chopped*

1. Preheat the oven to 325°F. Line a large rimmed baking sheet with parchment paper.

2. Add the cream, sugar, and golden syrup to a medium saucepan on medium heat. Cook just until it starts to bubble, stirring occasionally, until it is very lightly golden and smooth. Remove from the heat, add the butter, vanilla, salt, chile, orange blossom water, and orange zest, and stir continuously until the butter has melted. Stir in the toasted nuts and seeds until well combined, then quickly transfer the mixture to the prepared baking sheet. Use the back of a rubber spatula to spread out the mixture into a 16 x 12-inch/ 40 x 30 cm rectangle.

3. Bake for 10 minutes, then rotate the sheet and bake for 15 minutes more. Sprinkle evenly with the barberries, pushing them gently into the mix with the back of a spoon, and return to the oven for another 2 minutes. Set aside to cool completely, 30–45 minutes.

4. Meanwhile, temper the chocolate. Put the chocolate into a heatproof bowl set over a small saucepan of simmering water, with the bottom of the bowl not touching the water. Once two-thirds melts, remove the bowl from the heat and gently stir until the chocolate is completely smooth and melted (this helps the chocolate set at room temperature).

5. Drizzle the melted chocolate all over the surface of the brittle, then allow to set completely, about 30 minutes, or refrigerate to help it set faster. Break the brittle apart into randomly-sized large pieces and serve piled on a plate or board.

Make it your own:
- Play with the nuts and seeds, using more of less of either.
- Use other types of chocolate for drizzling.
- Bag and tie these up as a festive DIY gift!

Get ahead:
- Store in an airtight container for up to 1 week.

Sticky miso bananas with lime and toasted rice

Prep time: *5 minutes*
Cook time: *30 minutes*

This dessert ticks all our flavor boxes—sweet, salty, tangy, and umami—and all our texture boxes—sticky, crunchy, and creamy. The bananas you use should have almost completely yellow skin, with only the tiniest bit of brown spotting.

Serves 4

3 tbsp unsalted butter

packed ⅓ cup/70g light
   brown sugar

½ tsp ground star anise

3 tbsp crème fraîche

1½ tbsp white miso

4 medium bananas (*medium
   ripe*), *peeled and halved
   lengthwise*

1 lime: *finely grate the zest
   to get 1 tsp and then juice
   to get 1½ tsp*

TOASTED RICE TOPPING

1 tbsp Thai sticky rice
   (*raw*), *or jasmine rice*

2 tsp black sesame seeds

½ tsp ground star anise

1. Set the oven to its highest broil setting.

2. Make the topping. Toast the rice in a small frying pan on medium heat for 12–15 minutes, shaking the pan from time to time, until deeply golden. Blitz in a spice or coffee grinder until fine, then transfer to a small bowl. Return the pan to medium-high heat and add the sesame seeds. Toast for 1 minute, then stir into the rice bowl along with the star anise. Set aside.

3. Put the butter, sugar, star anise, and half the crème fraîche into a large, oven-safe cast-iron pan (or a large sauté pan) on medium heat. Stir the mixture frequently, until the butter has melted and the sugar has dissolved, then, off the heat, whisk in the miso until smooth.

Add the bananas, cut side up, using a spoon to coat the tops with some of the caramel, then transfer to the oven and broil for about 8 minutes (this will vary, depending on your broiler, so check them at the 7-minute mark), or until the bananas have softened and are lightly browned.

4. While the bananas are broiling, mix the remaining crème fraîche with the lime juice. When ready, spoon this all over the bananas, then sprinkle with the lime zest and 1 tablespoon of the rice topping. Serve immediately and directly from the pan, with the extra rice topping alongside.

> *Make it your own:*
> – No spice grinder? No problem! Swap out the ground rice for nuts, seeds, or dried coconut flakes.
>
> _____
>
> _____
>
> _____

VEG BOX

WHO DOES THE DISHES?

FRIDGE RAID

THAT ONE SHELF

FREEZER IS YOUR FRIEND

Index

Acknowledgments

If there's one thing that's apparent in these pages, and for any future stories that the Test Kitchen has to tell, it is that OTK is made up of a team of individuals who each bring to the table their unique quirks and attributes. We cook and bake, style and photograph, write and publish, but more than anything we work together and the OTK would not exist were it not for the efforts of everyone involved. Beyond this, we feel super lucky to have worked with a multitude of talents within their trade, and for this we extend our gratitude.

For the design, a massive thank you to Caz Hildebrand, the creative mastermind behind the edgy cover and whimsical book name *Shelf Love*. You truly brought our visions to life with your out-of-the-box thinking and daring splashes of color. And to Ashlea O'Neill for her design contribution as well. Also a big high five to Wei Tang, for your props, plants, and virtual hugs.

For the photography, many thanks to Elena Heatherwick and her partner in crime, Lesley Lau, who captured the Test Kitchen vibes so beautifully. They also provided plenty of giggles throughout the shoot and took home all the leftovers, and for this we are very appreciative.

We're super grateful to the team at Ebury, especially Celia Palazzo for leading the project and Emily Brickell for swiftly making sure we stayed on track. We also extend our thanks to Joel Rickett, Lizzy Gray, Sarah Bennie, Stephenie Naulls, Annie Lee, and Catherine Ngwong. Across continents we say a huge thank you to Aaron Wehner, Jennifer Sit, Kim Witherspoon, Maria Zizka, Jen Wang, Kim Tyner, Mark McCauslin, Windy Dorresteyn, Kate Tyler, and Jana Branson.

Much love and multiple hugs to the team at Gemma Bell, especially Gemma, Jen, and Millie, for adding such wonderful energy to the OTK momentum.

As always, thank you to Mark Hutchinson and Felicity Rubinstein for their support and guidance throughout.

To Nina Tolstrup, we are so grateful to have found you . . . and for the Test Kitchen makeover!

Lastly we'd like to thank Cornelia Staeubli and Noam Bar for their unconditional support in all things OTK.

Noor's acknowledgments

Thank you to my parents, Salah and Vanessa Murad, my two halves of two very different worlds whose unconditional love and support has shaped who I am today. And of course to my sister, Farah Murad.

A huge thanks to the OTK team: to Gitai Fisher, my work partner-in-crime turned brother, whose honesty and strength of character means he won't be rid of me anytime soon. The OTK would not be, were it not for you, habibti. To Verena Lochmuller, the most clever pastry chef I have come across, whose passion and talent speaks volumes. You put a smile on my face every day with your kindness, humor, and daily meows. To Ixta Belfrage, for being an all-round badass and a pleasure to learn from over the last 3 years. To Tara Wigley and Sami Tamimi, for letting me come into my own via team *Falastin*! To Chaya Pugh, whose jovial spirit brightens even the gloomiest of days. To Claudine Boulstridge, for her support from afar and her array of farm animal photos including pheasants, chicks, and llamas. To Cornelia, for finding my CV in her inbox many moons ago and for carving my place in the Ottolenghi family. To all the individuals who have left their mark at the Test Kitchen over the last decade, and all the influences yet to come: the OTK is, and always will be, an accumulation of voices harmoniously in sync.

Much love to my rock, Anosha Watson, who believes in me (a little bit) more than I believe in myself and pushes me (a lotta bit) beyond my own limitations. I don't know where I'd be without you.

To my oldest and dearest friend, Maram Jaberi, who I carry with me through every life event. Thank you to you and your family for instigating my lifelong love affair with Persian cuisine.

To Josh Meehan, the most rewarding surprise of 2020, thank you for your unwavering love and support.

To Celia, Joel, Emily, and the whole team at Ebury, many thanks for bringing the OTK vision to life.

To the creative stars Elena Heatherwick, Caz Hildebrand, Nina Tolstrup, and Wei Tang: it truly has been a pleasure working with you. The same goes to Gemma Bell and Jen, for being such an awesome force to work with and be around.

To my two London head chefs Shalom and Daniel, now friends for whom I have the utmost respect, thank you for taking a punt on this sassy girl from Bahrain.

Most importantly, a big shukran to Yotam, for being the beating heart of the Test Kitchen, an unwavering source of encouragement and inspiration, and a leader who will constantly strive to push his team forward.

Shelf Love notes

Published in Canada by Appetite by Random House®,
a division of Penguin Random House Canada Limited.

www.penguinrandomhouse.ca

Appetite by Random House® and colophon are registered trademarks
of Penguin Random House LLC.

Originally published in hardcover in Great Britain by Ebury Press,
an imprint of Ebury Publishing, a division of Penguin Random House Ltd.,
London, in 2021.

Library and Archives Canada Cataloguing in Publication is available upon
request.

ISBN: 978-0-525-61160-8
eBook ISBN: 978-0-525-61161-5

Design: Caz Hildebrand
Photography: Elena Heatherwick
Prop styling: Wei Tang
Printed in China

First Canadian Edition

10 9 8 7 6 5 4 3 2 1

appetite   Penguin
by RANDOM HOUSE   Random House
                        Canada

NON-VEG MAINS

Black lime beef skewers with sumac onions p. 52

Green herb bagna cauda p. 64

(All the) herb dumplings with caramelized onions p. 70

Spicy pulled pork vindaloo p. 110

Baked orzo puttanesca p. 114

Berbere spiced chicken, carrots, and chickpeas p. 117·

Za'atar salmon and tahini p. 119

Chickpeas cacio e pepe p. 120

One-pan crispy spaghetti and chicken p. 122

Braised beef short ribs with butter beans and figs p. 125

Sticky sweet and sour plums and sausages p. 131

Magical chicken and Parmesan soup with pappardelle p. 143

Celebration rice with lamb, chicken, and garlic yogurt p. 144

Fish koftas in ancho chile and tomato sauce p. 149

Mediterranean-style fried rice with anchovy lemon dressing p. 153

Rice koofteh in spiced tomato sauce p. 156

Cobb salad with mango and lime dressing p. 184

Buckwheat-battered fish with toum and pickled chiles p. 193

KID-FRIENDLY

Creamy dreamy hummus p. 20

Pita p. 23

Cheesy polenta and tomato sauce p. 24

Za'atar parathas with grated tomato p. 28

Chaat masala chickpea and polenta fries *(no onions or chiles)* p. 32

Yogurt rice with chana dal and curry leaf oil *(no chiles)* p. 42

Very giant giant couscous cake p. 48

Roasted potatoes with aïoli and buttered pine nuts p. 78

5-a-day toad-in-the-hole p. 106

Baked orzo puttanesca p. 114

Chickpeas cacio e pepe *(no chiles)* p. 120

One-pan crispy spaghetti and chicken p. 122

M.E. mac 'n' cheese with za'atar pesto *(pesto on the side)* p. 140

Celebration rice with lamb, chicken, and garlic yogurt p. 144

Rice koofteh in spiced tomato sauce p. 156

Beyond potato salad p. 165

Peas, tahini, and za'atar p. 182

Buckwheat-battered fish with toum and pickled chiles *(with yoghurt, no chiles)* p. 193

(That one bag of) mixed veggies and potato fritters with harissa *(with mayo or yogurt)* p. 196

Creamed corn stuffed peppers with pickled jalapeños *(no jalapeños)* p. 199

Carrot cake sandwich cookies p. 212

Coconut dream cake p. 216

Frozen berries for little humans p. 223

Verena's road trip cookies p. 224

Chocoflan p. 226

ONE POT/PAN/TRAY

UNDER AN HOUR